Contents

Introduction

Everyone has their favourite smell that reminds them of home ... mine is baking. My grandfather had a wood-burning oven built in his garden and many local people used to bring him simple ingredients like flour, yeast, salt and extra virgin olive oil, and he would make breads or pizza in exchange for some meats, fish or cheeses. I grew up making my own bread and I'm very pleased that I can now share this experience, along with all my other baking recipes with you.

There is nothing more satisfying than baking and I can tell you right now that it doesn't have to be complicated – as this book will prove. Next time you are shopping for breads or cakes, take a look at the back of the packet and you will see that there are at least 10–15 ingredients listed. Fresh home baking needs no more than 3–5 ingredients and will cost you next to nothing. From my book you will learn how to make various breads, cakes, biscuits, pizzas and pasta bakes that will take you and your family back in time so you too can experience the smells, flavours and textures of traditional Italian baking.

I'm sure you food-lovers will have experienced some of the more popular breads such as ciabatta and grissini, which originate from north Italy, focaccia, from central Italy, and the more rustic breads and, of course, pizzas from the south, where I come from. I'm going to teach you how to make these classics and many more and, once you have the basics, you can be as creative with fillings and toppings as you wish. Baking is great fun to do with kids and extremely impressive when inviting friends round for dinner ... have I convinced you yet?

I know some of you might feel daunted by home-baking but I am all about fresh simple ingredients. I have proved with my previous books that I keep things easy with few ingredients and I won't let you down with this latest collection... my motto still stands as always:

Minimum Effort, Maximum Satisfaction!

Enjoy and *Buon Appetito!*

ITALIAN HOME BAKING

Dedication

This book is dedicated to the most amazing woman I have ever met, Lina Vetere, for all the loyalty and strength you have shown me in the past eight years. Thank you for being a true friend.

GINO D'ACAMPO

ITALIAN HOME BAKING

Photography by Peter Cassidy

Kyle Books

First published in Great Britain in 2011 by
Kyle Books
23 Howland Street, London W1T 4AY
general.enquiries@kylebooks.com
www.kylebooks.com

10 9 8 7 6 5 4 3 2 1

ISBN 978-1-85626-978-0

Text © 2011 Gino D'Acampo
Book design © 2011 Kyle Books
Photographs © Peter Cassidy

Project editor: Jenny Wheatley
Photographer: Peter Cassidy
Designer: Jacqui Caulton
Food stylist: Lizzie Harris
Props stylist: Cynthia Inions
Make-up artist: Abbi-Rose Crook
Copy editor: Stephanie Evans
Production: Nic Jones and David Hearn

A Cataloguing In Publication record for this title is
available from the British Library.

Colour reproduction by Alta Image, London.
Printed and bound by C&C Offset in China.

Acknowledgements

A special thank you goes to my friend and manager Jeremy
Hicks for all the wisdom that he has shared with me in the
past eight years. Don't worry my friend, this time next year
we will be millionaires!

A big kiss to my long-term publisher Kyle Cathie for all the
trust and commitment you have shown me in the last five
books together – I am truly grateful.

To all the team who made this book look so beautiful; Peter,
Lizzie, Jenny, Jacqui, Cynthia and Abbi, you guys have
worked very hard and I really can't thank you enough.

A big thank you goes to all my colleagues and friends at
Bonta' Italia; Marco, Leo, Lina, Loredana and Franco for
always supporting me with my crazy projects. (Marco – of
course you are the best, my friend).

I'd like to thank my good friend Dino, master baker, for his
invaluable help with the bread recipes. Emilia and Domenico
of Masseria Storica Pilapalucci in Puglia were great hosts
on our location shoot and introduced us to two wonderful
bakeries in Altamura; La Panetta di Picerno G. Carlo and
Anticuus Fornus Sancta Clara di Vito Macella. The guys at
Altamura market were also good sports!

A massive *grazie* goes to my wife and best friend Jessie and
of course my two beautiful children, Rocco and Luciano;
remember boys, if you work hard in life you will achieve
everything you want.

The biggest thank you goes to all my fans, for once again
choosing my book; enjoy baking with me and *Buon Appetito!*

For more recipe ideas go to:

W www.ginodacampo.com

f facebook.com/ginodacampo

@ginofantastico

The story of baking in Italy

The Greeks taught the Romans how to bake leavened bread made of wheat flour around 170BC, and it soon became common for Roman households to keep a Greek baker at home who could bake up to 50 different kinds of bread using large wood fired ovens. This oven or *forno* is the cornerstone of baking in Italy. Up until 50 years ago, these ovens were often shared between families, who would take it in turns to bake their bread in the local *forno*. Over centuries, Italian baking has become extensive and diverse, with each region championing its own baking traditions, methods and ingredients. Italian baking encompasses everything from the very simple flatbreads, made from nothing but flour, water and salt, to pizzas and pasta bakes, right through to the most complex pastries. Today some of the most elaborate breads and pastries are prepared for religious celebrations. For instance, during Easter in Naples, where I'm from, it's common to find bread shaped into rings and baked with whole eggs in their shells to symbolise fertility and spring.

Types of bread

The most basic and most ancient kinds of Italian bread are flatbreads. Most are made without yeast which means that you don't need to knead them. If you've never made bread before, these are a good place to start! Flatbreads come in many regional varieties, such as *piada*, which is from Romagna and is traditionally made with flour, pig's fat (*ciccioli*), salt and water; and *crescia* or *torta al testo*, various forms of which originate from Le Marche and Umbria, and is traditionally cooked on a *testo*, a flat pan made from ground-up gravel and clay, and baked in a potter's kiln. They are normally eaten filled with cheese, such as pecorino or Parmesan, and salami or prosciutto.

Not all flatbreads are unleavened. The best known is focaccia. The bread dough is often mixed or spread with oil, herbs or onions, and is most certainly the ancestor of the pizza (another leavened flatbread). Flavourings vary between the regions; the Tuscan *schiacciata alla fiorentina* uses olive oil, rosemary, garlic or onion; while *focaccia Genovese* of Liguria typically includes herbs, sage, rosemary, oregano, onion and *ciccioli*. Meanwhile, *focaccia sud Barese* from Puglia is made from a very wet dough consisting chiefly of mashed potato. As you can see, there is plenty of flexibility to be had with ingredients and flavourings; in this book, I will teach you my own versions, including Stuffed Focaccia with Black Olives, Spinach and Mozzarella (see page 40).

One of the most well-known Italian breads is the ciabatta, which means 'slipper'. With its origins in Como in Liguria, the most important aspect of the method is that the dough needs to be very soft. In this book, I will teach you how to make the classic ciabatta, as well as a simple flavoured variation that uses purple olives and rosemary.

A baking lesson

In researching this book I visited a fantastic 50 square-metre antique wood oven in Altamura, Puglia, where focaccia and other breads and baked goods are still baked in the centuries-old tradition. A fire is built in the centre of the oven and when the wood burns down to embers it is moved to one side and the bread placed in the centre using a long paddle. The bread of Altamura is the most famous bread in Europe and is made from semolina (see page 15), and because it uses a starter dough or *biga* it has a tangy taste similar to sourdough bread. Altamura bread must be made from local flour and not imported! Originally these loaves were made to a size of 5kg so as to feed a family for a week. These days, people eat less bread than they used to and the loaves are a more manageable size of 1kg. The unique shape of the loaf means that the inside stays fresh for up to a week. When it starts to go hard it can be sliced and put in the oven with a slice of pecorino on top. It was also used to make *cialled* – in local dialect this means a broth that uses old bread – a similar concept to *pappa pomodoro* and good hearty peasant food. The baker at Sancta Clara gave me a lesson in cooking bread and focaccia, which in that region is cooked with tomatoes, oregano and salt.

Pizza

Focaccia is most certainly the ancestor of the pizza. Naples is generally seen as the birthplace of pizza in its current form as the peasants and working class of the city appreciated the way it allowed them to incorporate yesterday's leftovers, and the fact that it could be eaten without utensils. The word 'pizza' has an uncertain origin, but is generally understood to be the Neapolitan word for a tart with a flat pastry base and rolled puff pastry border. The renowned *pizza alla Napoletana* was the favoured fast food on the streets of 19th century Naples. While you can find variations of this pizza all over the world, Neapolitans take great pride in the authentic version, its soft dough with a raised *cornicione* (crust) around its edge, and the beautiful simplicity of its toppings, which in the case of *pizza alla Napoletana* is limited to fresh or tinned San Marzano tomatoes, garlic, fresh oregano or basil, salt and olive oil.

Over time, different regions in Italy have put their stamp on the pizza. If you've ever visited Rome, you'll probably be familiar with the thin and crispy base of the Roman pizza, which is divided into 6ft-long strips, and seasoned simply with olive oil and salt, or tomato and mozzarella. In Puglia, there is the *panzarotti*, a small closed pizza or calzone produced with soft dough and commonly filled with tomatoes and mozzarella; spinach, mushrooms, baby corn, and ham are also often used. Other fillings include onions stir fried in olive oil and seasoned with salted anchovies and capers.

Pasta

Remember the last time you indulged in a *lasagne al forno*, the classic lasagne consisting of flat sheets of cooked pasta layered with bechamel sauce and *ragù Bolognese*, and sprinkled with Parmesan. Nice feeling isn't it? Here I will teach you how to make a variety of baked pasta dishes, including my vegetarian version of lasagne (see page 153), and others using pastas cannelloni, fusilli, gnocchi, orecchiette and rigatoni. Aside from lasagne, you'll probably be familiar with cannelloni, which are large rolled sheets of pasta containing assorted fillings, and baked in a sauce (see page 152 for my version); and maccheroni, which is baked in a shallow dish with cheese or a tomato and cheese sauce. My version on page 150, which uses four cheeses, is probably as cheesy and creamy as it gets.

Cakes and biscuits

A book on Italian baking wouldn't be complete without Italy's assortment of baked sweet offerings. You will learn how to make everything from amaretti and biscotti to cantuccini and panettone. Again, many of these sweet specialities bear regional variations. Amaretti biscuits are normally made from sweet and bitter almonds which are ground or chopped, mixed with beaten egg whites and sugar, then baked (see my version on page 132). In Sardinia, amaretti are made from pulverised almonds stirred into the beaten egg whites to form a lighter, meringue-like biscuit.

A favourite to be dunked in morning espressos and cappuccinos, biscotti means 'twice cooked'. Many Italian versions are made by first cooking the mixture in a narrow loaf shape, then letting it cool and cutting it into diagonal slices which are then cooked again at a lower temperature to make them dry and crisp. There is quite a bit of latitude in the way biscotti is made. Some versions use butter or oil, while others do not; eggs are also an optional ingredient. In this book, I've provided simple but delicious recipes that use a combination of fruit (see page 136) and spices (see page 139). Other popular versions you might come across include *biscotti al latte*, made with butter, eggs, milk, honey, sugar, lemon and orange zest, and vanilla; and *biscottini all'anice* which uses anise. Another twice-cooked biscuit, cantuccini typically consist of chopped toasted almonds, flour, and egg yolks beaten with sugar, and traditionally form the sweet ending of a meal in Tuscany. Again, there is some flexibility in what goes into a great batch of cantuccini. My version (see page 140) uses pistachios alongside almonds, and is flavoured by a dash of vanilla.

Perhaps the single most important festive cake is panettone. Despite its light but firm texture, this large domed cake, served over the Christmas period, is packed full of flavour as it brims with dried fruit and candied peel, and the fragrance of vanilla and liqueurs. Panettones have been mass produced in Milan, their birthplace, since the 1920s. Making panettone at home is no mean feat, needing several lengthy risings in just the right conditions, as one false step taking it out of the dome-like mould can lead to your cake collapsing. In this book, I take the intimidation out of baking panettone with an easy-to-follow, classic recipe on page 96 – and you don't have to wait until Christmas to try it! You can also take this cake one step further by turning it into a delicious Panettone and Butter Pudding – see my recipe on 98.

Baking essentials

There are no hard and fast rules with Italian baking. Different bakers, including my friend Dino (pictured above), who helped me to develop several of the recipes in this book, will prefer to use certain flours to make breads and cakes over others. In this book, I have mainly used strong white flour for making breads and pizza bases, and plain or self-raising flour for cakes and biscuits. Here are some definitions of other flours and baking essentials to help you on your way.

Strong white flour – This flour is made from hard wheat which has a high protein content and therefore contains extra gluten. This enables the dough to stretch as the yeast acts, making this type of flour particularly good for bread-making. It is also sometimes labelled as 'bread flour'.

'00' flour – In Italy, flour is available in grades of '00', '0', '1', and '2' according to how finely ground it is. *'Doppia zero'* or '00' flour is the finest and whitest, and is best known for making pasta, but in Italy it is used for making cakes and bread, too.

Plain flour – This flour is low in gluten and so is ideal for making cakes and pastries, but should not be used for making bread. It is not found in Italy but Italians would use '00' flour for the same purpose as it is also finely milled.

Self-raising flour – This is plain flour that has a raising agent (baking powder) added to it. Self-raising flour is not used in Italy – we would instead use '00' flour with baking powder added to it.

Semolina – Known as *semola* in Italy, this is hard durum wheat that has been ground into a flour. Don't confuse it with the British milk pudding! Semolina usually has a coarse texture and a pale yellow colour and is used mainly in southern Italy for making pizza, biscuits, gnocchi and of course, bread. Semolina is available as a coarse or fine flour and can be found in your local supermarket or health-food store.

Wholemeal flour – Traditionally consumed by the working classes in Italy, wholemeal flour has been gaining popularity among artisan bakers as it adds additional flavour to breads. It is a good option for people who would like to follow a high-fibre diet.

Rye flour – Rye grows well in colder regions and is commonly used for baking in northern Italy. It is high in fibre and has lower gluten levels than wheat, so is often mixed with strong white flour for bread making.

Yeast – I use fast-action dried yeast in most of the recipes in this book for ease, but if you prefer you can use double the amount of fresh. Fresh yeast is not as easy to find but but is often available from health-food stores or the bakeries in some supermarkets. Dry yeast keeps well in the storecupboard, but do keep an eye on its expiry date! The advantage of fast-action or easy-blend dried yeast is that you don't need to add water or sugar to activate it.

Water – The purity and temperature of the water you use in your baking can make all the difference to its quality. Bakers in Italy swear that the local water they use gives their bread its distinctive taste, meaning it cannot be reproduced elsewhere. The temperature of the water should be similar to that of your hand, about 22–24°C.

How to knead bread dough

Kneading is one of the most important processes in making bread. Without getting too technical you need to evenly distribute the yeast so the dough rises evenly. The texture you are looking for is quite tight and stretchy. Under-kneading will leave the dough soggy while over-kneading (normally only a likelihood if you are using a food-processor fitted with a dough hook) will result in a bread with large holes in it. There are no better tools for kneading than your hands.

1 The most important thing to remember before you start kneading is that it's best to work your bread dough in a warm place, just like professional bakers do in their shops.

2 Place all the dry ingredients in a bowl (I prefer stainless steel). Then add the liquids and mix together using a wooden spoon.

3 Dust your working area with plenty of flour.

4 Rub a little olive oil into your hands to prevent the dough from sticking to them.

5 Gather the dough mixture into a ball shape (adding a little more flour if sticky or little more liquid if crumbly).

6 Transfer the dough ball onto your floured surface and fold in half.

7 Using the palm of your hand push the dough away from you a couple of times. Give the dough a quarter turn, fold in half and repeat the process of pushing the dough away from you.

8 Use a scraper to collect any dough that sticks to the work surface. The dough will gradually become easier to work with, the more you knead it.

9 Continue to knead the dough until its texture is elastic and smooth. The process should take about 10–15 minutes. (As a guide, pinch the dough and if it is ready it should feel like your earlobe.)

Gino's top 10 baking tips

1 Always use good weighing scales or accurate measuring jugs.

2 Whatever ingredients you use, for example milk, eggs, butter and water – ensure they are all at room temperature.

3 Use good-quality non-stick tins and, when baking cakes or biscuits, line them with greaseproof paper.

4 Leaving a dough to rise before baking makes the loaf springy and airy. Rising or proving should always be done in a draught-free, warm place.

5 If you are adding any extra flavours to the bread dough, do so at the last folding stage.

6 If you want your bread to develop a good crust, spray the oven 10 times with water from a spray bottle before you start baking.

7 Most baking should be done in the middle of a preheated oven. A dish that requires more than 30 minutes' cooking should normally be baked in a low oven, whereas a dish that requires less than 30 minutes tends to need baking in a high oven.

8 To test if a cake is cooked, insert a cocktail stick or strand of raw spaghetti in the centre. If it comes out clean, the cake is ready.

9 Once your cake or tart is baked, let it rest for at least 3 minutes at room temperature before turning it out of the tin. This will prevent it breaking and make your life easier when portioning.

10 When making baked pasta dishes, you must ensure that the pasta is cooked al dente (still with a little 'bite'), otherwise it will become soggy and sticky when it is baked in the oven.

BREADS

CIABATTA CLASSICA
Ciabatta bread

One of the most famous of Italian breads, and one that can be created in your own home – with a little bit of time and love. You can't beat a traditional homemade ciabatta and this recipe is really simple as well as scrumptious. The authentic techniques of slowly fermenting the dough and handcrafting it into the characteristic slipper shape gives this classic bread its bubbly open texture and distinctive golden crust. Ideal to accompany any cheese board or simply serve it dipped into good-quality extra virgin olive oil.

Makes 4 'slippers'

FOR THE STARTER (BIGA)

350g strong white flour

180ml water, warm

5g fresh yeast

FOR THE DOUGH

450g strong white flour
    plus extra for dusting

10g fresh yeast

340ml water, warm

50ml extra virgin olive oil
    plus extra for brushing

1 teaspoon salt

1   To prepare the starter or *biga,* place all the ingredients in a large bowl and mix by hand for 5 minutes to form a rough dough. Brush the inside of the bowl with oil, place the dough inside, cover with clingfilm and leave the starter to rest away from draughts overnight.

2   Next day, make the dough: sift the flour into a large bowl and rub in the yeast. Scoop out the starter that you previously prepared and add to the bowl with the flour and yeast. Pour in the water and oil, add the salt and mix well until fully combined. Transfer to a lightly floured surface and knead the dough for 8 minutes until you have a smooth ball.

3   Brush the inside of another large bowl with oil and place the dough ball in it. Cover the bowl with clingfilm and leave it to rise in a warm place away from draughts for 1½ hours until bubbly and light.

4   Transfer the dough to a floured surface and sprinkle a little flour on top. Gently press down with your fingers and divide into 4 equal strips. Fold one side of your flattened dough into the middle, then bring the other side over to the middle and press down to seal. Finally, fold in half lengthways and seal the edges to create a long shape.

5   Cover a flat baking sheet with a tea towel and sprinkle it with flour.

6   Place the four dough strips on the tea towel, cover with another tea towel and leave to rest in a warm place away from draughts for 40 minutes.

7   Flour a baking tray and preheat the oven to 220°C/gas mark 7.

8   Pick up one ciabatta, turn it over and lay on the floured baking tray. Gently stretch the ciabatta lengthways to give the characteristic 'slipper' shape. Repeat with the remaining three.

9   Spray the inside of the oven with water (see page 15) and bake the ciabatta in the middle of the oven for 20 minutes until beautiful and golden.

10 Serve warm and enjoy.

CIABATTA CON OLIVE E ROSMARINO
Ciabatta with purple olives and rosemary

Enriching the dough with extra virgin olive oil gives a fragrant flavour and silky mouth-feel; adding olives and rosemary will send you to heaven and back. The saltiness of the olives combined with the freshness of the rosemary will not disappoint. For maximum satisfaction, do use good-quality olives. If you are serving a bland starter or a simple soup, accompany it with this ciabatta and everyone will want more (in fact, always make double portions of this bread!)

Makes 4 'slippers'

FOR THE STARTER (BIGA)

350g strong white flour

180ml water, warm

5g fresh yeast

FOR THE DOUGH

450g strong white flour
    plus extra for dusting

10g fresh yeast

340ml water, warm

50ml extra virgin olive oil
    plus extra for brushing

180g pitted Kalamata olives,
    quartered

2 tablespoons rosemary leaves,
    finely chopped

1 teaspoon salt

1 To prepare the starter or *biga,* place all the ingredients in a large bowl and mix by hand for 5 minutes to form a rough dough. Brush the inside of the bowl with oil, cover with clingfilm and leave the starter to rest away from draughts overnight.

2 Next day, make the dough: sift the flour into a large bowl and rub in the yeast. Scoop out the starter that you previously prepared and add to the bowl with the flour and yeast. Pour in the water with the oil and salt. Transfer to a lightly floured surface and knead the dough for 8 minutes until you have a smooth ball.

3 Brush the inside of another large bowl with oil and place the dough ball in it. Cover with clingfilm and leave it to rise in a warm place away from draughts for 1½ hours until bubbly and light.

4 Transfer the dough to a floured surface and sprinkle a little flour on top. Gently press down with your fingers and divide into 4 equal strips. Scatter over the olives and rosemary. Fold one side of your flattened dough into the middle, than bring the other side over to the middle and press down to seal. Finally, fold in half lengthways and seal the edges to create a long shape.

5 Cover a flat baking sheet with a tea towel and sprinkle it with flour.

6 Place the four dough strips on the tea towel, cover with another tea towel and leave to rest in a warm place away from draughts for 40 minutes.

7 Flour a baking tray and preheat the oven to 220°C/gas mark 7.

8 Pick up one ciabatta, turn it over and lay on the floured baking tray. Gently stretch the ciabatta lengthways to give the characteristic 'slipper' shape. Repeat with the remaining three.

9 Spray the inside of the oven with water (see page 15) and bake the ciabatta in the middle of the oven for 20 minutes until golden.

10 Serve warm to accompany a platter of mixed antipasti.

CIAMBELLONE
Italian-style cottage loaf

A simple bread (only five ingredients) that requires no more than 40 minutes to cook. What more do you want? You now have no excuses, so head for the kitchen and get baking! My *ciambellone,* after it has cooled to room temperature, will last for at least four days if wrapped in a plastic bag. On the fourth day, if any that remains is too hard, slice it, toast it and spread with a little butter and your favourite jam.

Makes 1 large round loaf

680g strong white flour
   plus extra for dusting
2 teaspoons salt
10g fast-action dried yeast
400ml water, warm
Olive oil for brushing

1 Brush 2 baking trays with oil.

2 Mix the flour, salt and yeast in a large bowl and make a well in the centre. Pour in the water and mix to form a firm dough. If necessary add a little more flour.

3 Transfer the dough to a lightly floured surface and knead for 10 minutes until smooth and elastic. Brush the inside of another bowl with oil and place the dough inside. Cover with clingfilm and leave to rise in a warm place away from draughts for 1 hour.

4 Turn out the dough onto a lightly floured surface and punch down. Knead for 3 minutes then divide into two-thirds and one-third, shape each into a ball and place on the oiled baking trays. Brush the tops with a little oil and cover with clingfilm. Leave the dough to rise in a warm, draught-free place for a further 30 minutes.

5 Preheat the oven to 220°C/gas mark 7.

6 Gently flatten the top of the larger round and use a sharp knife to cut a 4cm cross in the centre. Brush with a little water and place the smaller round on top.

7 Using the thumb and the first two fingers of one hand, press a hole down through the centre of the top ball, right into the lower one. Brush the lot with a little oil, cover with clingfilm and leave to rest for 8 minutes.

8 Bake on the bottom of the oven for 40 minutes until the loaf is beautifully golden all over.

9 Transfer to a wire rack to cool slightly and serve warm.

FILONE ALL'ARRABBIATA
Spicy loaf with chilli and cayenne pepper

Hot, hot, hot! That's what this bread is all about. A spicy crusty loaf that will have you and your friends begging for more. Delicious with any cheese, or served with a simple soup. I find it easier to use dried chilli flakes instead of chopped fresh chilli as the flakes blend better with the dough. You can, if you prefer, substitute smoked paprika for the cayenne pepper.

Makes 1 loaf

225g strong white flour
100g wholemeal flour
1 teaspoon salt
7g fast-action dried yeast
210ml water, warm
2 tablespoons extra virgin olive oil
   plus extra for brushing
3 teaspoons dried chilli flakes
1 teaspoon cayenne pepper

1 Brush a baking tray and the inside of a large bowl with oil.

2 Mix the flours, salt and yeast together in another large bowl and make a well in the centre. Pour in the water with the oil and mix to create a soft dough.

3 Transfer the dough to a lightly floured surface and knead for 10 minutes until smooth and elastic. Shape it into a ball and place in the oiled bowl. Cover with clingfilm and leave it to rise in a warm place away from draughts for 1 hour.

4 Turn out the dough onto a lightly floured surface and punch down. Flatten out and sprinkle over the chilli flakes and cayenne pepper. Fold up and knead again for 3 minutes. Shape into an oval loaf, place onto the oiled baking tray and leave to rest for 5 minutes.

5 Use a sharp knife to make five diagonal cuts on the top of the loaf. Brush the top with a little oil and cover with clingfilm. Leave it to rise in a warm place away from draughts for 40 minutes.

6 Preheat the oven to 200°C/gas mark 6.

7 Brush the top of the loaf with more oil and bake in the middle of the oven for 35 minutes.

8 Transfer to a wire rack to cool slightly and serve warm to accompany your favourite dips, cheese or enjoy with soup.

FILONE RUSTICO CON OLIVE
Rustic loaf with black and green olives

Filone is popular throughout Italy, as an everyday bread. It is likened to the baguette (only shorter and fatter) and especially suits rich dishes, such as hearty stews and casseroles. I have added olives for even more flavour but you can leave them out if you prefer. *Scarpetta* is the word used to describe the action of mopping up any leftover sauces, and it is almost as if the *filone* was designed for this purpose alone – rather like a sponge, it is superb at absorbing even the richest of sauces!

Makes 1 loaf

225g strong white flour

100g wholemeal flour

1 teaspoon salt

½ teaspoon freshly ground
black pepper

7g fast-action dried yeast

210ml water, warm

2 tablespoons extra virgin olive oil
plus extra for brushing

70g pitted green olives, roughly
chopped

70g pitted Kalamata olives,
roughly chopped

1   Brush a baking tray and the inside of a large bowl with oil.

2   Mix the flours, salt, pepper and yeast together in another large bowl and make a well in the centre. Pour in the water with the oil and mix until you have a soft dough.

3   Transfer the dough to a lightly floured surface and knead for 10 minutes until smooth and elastic. Shape it into a ball and place in the oiled bowl. Cover with clingfilm and leave it to rise in a warm place away from draughts for 1 hour.

4   Turn out the dough onto a lightly floured surface and punch down. Flatten it out and sprinkle over the olives. Fold up and knead again for 2 minutes. Leave the dough to rest for 5 minutes then shape into an oval loaf and place on the oiled baking tray.

5   Use a sharp knife to make five diagonal cuts on the top of the loaf. Brush the top with a little oil and cover with clingfilm. Leave to rise in a warm place away from draughts for 40 minutes.

6   Preheat the oven to 200°C/gas mark 6.

7   Brush the top of the loaf with more oil and bake in the middle of the oven for 35 minutes.

8   Transfer to a wire rack to cool slightly and serve warm or at room temperature.

PANE RUSTICO
Rustic north Italian bread

This bread is especially good paired with a Parmesan or other strong cheese and salami.

Makes 2 round loaves

400g strong white flour
100g wholemeal flour
1½ teaspoons sea salt
½ teaspoon caster sugar
7g fast-action dried yeast
270ml water
10ml extra virgin olive oil

1 Place the flours in a large bowl, add the sea salt, sugar and yeast, and mix all the ingredients together.

2 Add the water and extra virgin olive oil to the dry ingredients and mix together. To make this easier you could start by using a wooden spoon, continue until all the ingredients come together then transfer the mixture to a floured surface and finish kneading by hand for about 10–15 minutes or until the dough becomes smooth and silky.

3 At this point the dough is ready to rest. Put the dough into an oiled bowl, cover with clingfilm and leave it to rise in a warm place away from draughts for 2½–3 hours or until doubled in size.

4 Turn out the dough onto a lightly floured surface and punch down. Divide it into 2 equal pieces and work both of them on a floured work surface, trying to get a loose, rounded shape. Place them on a baking tray, cover with a damp tea towel and leave to rest for 1 hour or until doubled in size.

5 Preheat the oven to 180°C/gas mark 4.

6 Use a sharp knife to make a deep cut in a shape of a cross on the top of the loaves.

7 If you have a water spray bottle, use this to spray the oven sides before placing the baking tray in the middle of the oven (this creates steam and will give colour and a nice crust to your bread – see page 15 – but don't worry if you don't have one). Bake for about 20 minutes, until the loaves are uniformly golden in colour.

PANE TOSCANO
Tuscan-style bread

As Tuscan bread is well known for being low in salt it is best served with strong-flavoured foods such as salami, cheeses, or a hearty bean soup.

Makes 2 long loaves

500g strong white flour
½ teaspoon sea salt
1 teaspoon caster sugar
7g fast-action dried yeast
300ml water

1   Place the flour in a large bowl, add the sea salt, sugar and yeast, and mix all the ingredients together.

2   Add the water and mix together. To make this easier you could start by using a wooden spoon, continue until all the ingredients come together then transfer the mixture to a floured surface and finish kneading by hand for about 10–15 minutes or until the dough becomes smooth and silky.

3   At this point the dough is ready to rest. Put the dough into an oiled bowl, cover with clingfilm and leave it to rise in a warm place away from draughts for 1–2 hours or until doubled in size.

4   Turn out the dough onto a lightly floured surface and punch down. Divide it into 2 equal square pieces and flatten both of them to a thickness of about 2.5cm then, as if making a Swiss roll, start to roll the dough loosely from one end until you have something that looks like a loaf. Place them on a lightly floured baking tray, cover with a damp tea towel to prevent the surface of the dough from drying out. Leave to rest for 1 hour or until doubled in volume.

5   Preheat the oven to 180°C/gas mark 4.

6   Use a sharp knife to gently score the loaves straight down the middle.

7   If you have a water spray bottle, use this to spray the oven sides before placing the baking tray in the middle of the oven (this creates steam and will give colour and a nice crust to your bread – see page 15 – but don't worry if you don't have one). Bake for about 20 minutes, until the loaves are uniformly golden in colour.

FOCACCIA CLASSICA AL ROSMARINO

Classic rosemary focaccia

The satisfaction that comes from making bread is infinite ... from the moment that enticing aroma starts to fill the house, you can't beat the warm feeling you get from having created your very own piece of art and the immense pride that follows when your loved ones proclaim 'This is so tasty, I can't believe you made it!' Focaccia is a delicious classic bread that speaks for itself – one of my favourite Italian breads of all time – and is perfect on its own as well as served with a starter or main course.

Serves about 10

500g strong white flour
plus extra for dusting

7g fast-action dried yeast

6 tablespoons extra virgin olive oil
plus extra for brushing

300ml water, warm

2 teaspoons fine salt

1 tablespoon sea salt

2 tablespoons fresh
rosemary leaves

1 Brush a baking tray and the inside of a large bowl with oil.

2 Sift the flour into a large bowl and stir in the yeast. Make a well in the centre and pour in 3 tablespoons of the oil with the water. Add in the fine salt and with the help of a wooden spoon, mix together until all the ingredients are well combined.

3 Transfer the mixture to a lightly floured surface and knead for 10 minutes until you have a smooth and elastic dough. The dough should be soft; if it's really sticky, add a little more flour.

4 Fold the edges of the dough underneath to form a smooth rounded top. Place the dough in the oiled bowl and brush the top with a little more oil to prevent a crust from forming. Cover with clingfilm and leave to rise in a warm place away from draughts for 1 hour until doubled in size.

5 Slide the dough onto the oiled baking tray. Use your fingertips to make indentations in the dough while flattening it into an oval shape about 3cm thick, brush over a little oil and cover with clingfilm. Leave it to rise in a warm place away from draughts for 40 minutes until doubled in size.

6 Preheat the oven to 220°C/gas mark 7.

7 Once the dough has risen, gently press your fingertips into the dough to make more indentations. Tuck the rosemary leaves into the surface, sprinkle with the sea salt and drizzle 3 tablespoons of oil all over.

8 Bake in the middle of the oven for 20 minutes until beautifully golden. Once cooked, allow to cool slightly on a wire rack so that the focaccia does not sweat underneath. Serve it warm.

FOCACCIA ALLA PUTTANESCA
Focaccia topped with tomato, anchovies and capers

How can you have a party without a little focaccia to serve with your cocktails? Come on guys, this is the ultimate party food and once you have tried and experienced how easy it is to make, you will do it over and over again. Experiment with any topping of your choice and serve it warm to appreciate all the flavours together. Give it a go – you may also start your first love affair with anchovies!

Serves about 10

500g strong white flour
plus extra for dusting

7g fast-action dried yeast

6 tablespoons extra virgin olive oil
plus extra for brushing

300ml water, warm

2 teaspoons fine salt

300g passata (sieved tomatoes)

20 pitted Kalamata olives

20 anchovies fillets in oil, drained

1 tablespoon salted capers, rinsed
under cold water

2 teaspoons dried oregano

½ teaspoon dried chilli flakes

1 Brush a baking tray and the inside of a large bowl with oil.

2 Sift the flour into a large bowl and stir in the yeast. Make a well in the centre and pour in 3 tablespoons of the oil with the water. Add in the fine salt and with the help of a wooden spoon, mix together until all the ingredients are well combined.

3 Transfer the mixture to a lightly floured surface and knead for 10 minutes until you have a smooth and elastic dough. The dough should be soft; if it's really sticky, add a little more flour.

4 Fold the edges of the dough underneath to form a smooth rounded top. Place the dough in the oiled bowl and brush the top with a little more oil to prevent a crust from forming. Cover with clingfilm and leave to rise in a warm place away from draughts for 1 hour until doubled in size.

5 Slide the dough onto the oiled baking tray. Use your fingertips to make indentations in the dough while flattening it into an oval shape about 3cm thick, brush over a little oil and cover with clingfilm. Leave it to rise in a warm place away from draughts for 40 minutes until doubled in size.

6 Preheat the oven to 220°C/gas mark 7.

7 Once the dough has risen, gently press your fingertips into the dough to make more indentations. Spread over the passata to within 1cm of the edges. Scatter over the olives, anchovies and capers. Sprinkle the oregano and chilli flakes all over and finally drizzle the top with the remaining extra virgin olive oil.

8 Bake in the middle of the oven for 20 minutes until golden and beautiful. Once cooked, allow to slightly cool on a wire rack so that the focaccia cannot sweat underneath. Cut into 10 slices and serve warm with a cold beer.

FOCACCIA CON PANCETTA E CIPOLLE

Focaccia with crispy pancetta and onions

A simple dimple-topped bread that never fails to impress me. The combination of pancetta with onions is simply delicious. Serve my focaccia warm as a starter, with a few slices of salami. *Buonissimo!*

Serves about 10

2 tablespoons salted butter

250g diced pancetta

1 large onion, finely chopped

500g strong white flour
   plus extra for dusting

7g fast-action dried yeast

6 tablespoons extra virgin olive oil
   plus extra for brushing

300ml water, warm

2 teaspoons fine salt

1 tablespoon sea salt

1 Brush a baking tray and the inside of a large bowl with oil.

2 Melt the butter in a large frying pan over a medium heat and fry the pancetta and onions for 10 minutes, stirring occasionally. Set aside.

3 Sift the flour into a large bowl and stir in the yeast. Make a well in the centre and pour in 3 tablespoons of the oil with the water. Add in the fine salt and with the help of a wooden spoon, mix together until all the ingredients are well combined.

4 Transfer the mixture to a lightly floured surface and knead for 10 minutes until you have a smooth and elastic dough. The dough should be soft; if it's really sticky, add a little more flour.

5 Fold the edges of the dough underneath to form a smooth rounded top. Place the dough in the oiled bowl and brush the top with a little more oil to prevent a crust from forming. Cover with clingfilm and leave to rise in a warm place away from draughts for 1 hour until doubled in size.

6 Slide the dough onto the oiled baking tray. Gently fold the pancetta and onions into the dough for 2 minutes.

7 Use your fingertips to make indentations in the dough while flattening it into an oval shape about 3cm thick, brush over a little oil and cover with clingfilm. Leave it to rise in a warm place away from draughts for 40 minutes until doubled in size.

8 Preheat the oven to 220°C/gas mark 7.

9 Once the dough has risen, gently press your fingertips into the dough to make more indentations. Drizzle 3 tablespoons of oil all over and sprinkle with the sea salt.

10 Bake in the middle of the oven for 20 minutes until golden all over. Once cooked, allow to cool slightly on a wire rack so that the focaccia will not sweat underneath. Serve warm.

FOCACCIA RIPIENA
Stuffed focaccia with black olives, spinach and mozzarella

I love this bread; it's almost a meal in itself and could almost pass for a pizza with all the flavours I have put inside. You can be as creative as you like here and add in almost anything but the melted cheese with the strong flavour of the olives works perfectly with the spinach. This focaccia can be eaten warm or at room temperature and a slice will always be welcome in a lunchbox or on a picnic.

Serves 6

450g strong white flour

10g fast-action dried yeast

4 tablespoons extra virgin olive oil plus extra for brushing

300ml water, warm

Sea salt for sprinkling

Salt and pepper to taste

FOR THE FILLING

250g frozen spinach, defrosted

200g mozzarella cheese, chopped

20 pitted Kalamata olives, halved lengthways

2 teaspoons fresh rosemary leaves

1   Brush a 25cm loose-based cake tin and the inside of a large bowl with oil.

2   Sift the flour into a large bowl and stir in the yeast. Make a well in the centre, pour in the oil and the water and with the help of a wooden spoon, mix together until all the ingredients are well combined.

3   Transfer the mixture on a floured surface and knead for 10 minutes until you have a smooth and elastic dough. The dough should be soft; if it's really sticky, add a little more flour.

4   Place the dough in the oiled bowl, cover with clingfilm and leave to rise in a warm place away from draughts for about 1 hour until doubled in size.

5   Meanwhile, squeeze the spinach to remove any excess water and place in a large bowl. Add in the mozzarella, olives and rosemary. Season with salt and pepper and mix well.

6   Preheat the oven to 220°C/gas mark 7.

7   Punch down the dough and divide into 2 equal pieces. Roll out the first piece a little larger than the tin. Place on the base of the tin and try to mould the sides higher than the base. Spread the spinach mixture over the base to within 1cm of the edges.

8   Roll out the remaining dough to the same size as the tin, brush the edges with a little water and place over the filling. Press the edges together really well to ensure a good seal.

9   Gently press your fingertips into the dough to make more indentations then brush with extra virgin olive oil. Sprinkle with the sea salt and bake in the middle of the oven for 30 minutes until risen and firm.

10 Remove from the oven and leave to rest into the tin for 10 minutes on a wire rack allowing the air to circulate all around it.

11 Serve and enjoy while still warm and fragrant.

FOCACCIA DI RECCO
Stuffed focaccia with cheeses

La focaccia di Recco, typical of Liguria, can be eaten straight from the oven while the hot cheese is lovely and stringy or if you have any leftovers you can pop some ham in the middle and toast it. Either way, served with a fresh tomato and basil salad, it's delicious! This is another good focaccia to take on picnics or to provide something a little different for your children's lunchboxes.

Makes 1 round loaf

500g strong white flour

2 teaspoons sea salt

1 teaspoon caster sugar

5g fast-action dried yeast

2 tablespoons extra virgin olive oil plus extra for brushing

350ml water, warm

FOR THE FILLING

3 tablespoons extra virgin olive oil

75g extra mature Cheddar cheese cut into 2cm cubes

75g pearl mozzarella

1 Brush a 30cm pizza tray and the inside of a large bowl with oil.

2 Sift the flour into a large bowl and add the sea salt, sugar and yeast. Mix all the dry ingredients together. Make a well in the centre, pour in the oil and water and with the help of a wooden spoon, mix together until all the ingredients are well combined.

3 Transfer the mixture on a floured surface and knead for 10 minutes until you have a smooth and elastic dough. The dough should be soft; if it's really sticky, add a little more flour.

4 Place the dough in the oiled bowl, cover with clingfilm and leave to rise in a warm place away from draughts for about 2 hours until it has at least doubled in size.

5 When the dough is well risen, divide into 2 equal pieces and shape into round balls. Leave to rest for a further 10 minutes.

6 Roll out one ball of dough thinly, place on the oiled pizza tray and brush with oil. Sprinkle over the cubed Cheddar and pearl mozzarella. Then roll out the second ball of dough to the same size and place on top. Brush with the remaining oil.

7 Use your fingertips to gently press the dough down, making indentations on the surface of the focaccia. (It's fine if bits of cheese poke through, but do ensure that the edges are properly sealed to prevent the cheese from oozing out.) Leave to rise for 40 minutes.

8 Preheat the oven to 180°C/gas mark 4.

9 Prick the surface of the focaccia with a fork and bake for 15–20 minutes until it is golden brown in colour. Remove from the oven and serve.

PANE PUGLIESE
Semolina bread

This bread is a great choice for making bruschetta, drizzled with extra virgin olive oil and topped with cherry tomatoes, a pinch of oregano and sea salt.

Makes 2 oval loaves

350g strong white flour
   plus extra for dusting
150g fine semolina
2 teaspoons sea salt
1 teaspoon caster sugar
7g fast-action dried yeast
350ml water, warm

1 Brush the inside of a large bowl with oil.

2 Place the flour and semolina in a large bowl and add the salt, sugar and yeast. Mix all the dry ingredients together.

3 Make a well in the centre, pour in the water and with the help of a wooden spoon, mix together until all the ingredients are well combined.

4 Transfer the mixture on a floured surface and knead for 10–15 minutes until you have a smooth and elastic dough. The dough should be soft and silky; if it's really sticky, add a little more flour.

5 Place the dough in the oiled bowl, cover with clingfilm and leave to rise in a warm place away from draughts for about 2 hours until it has at least doubled in size.

6 Divide the dough into 2 equal pieces, and work each of these on a floured work surface, trying to make a loose, rounded shape, then leave to rest again for 30–40 minutes.

7 Take the dough and gently flatten both rounds until they are slightly larger in shape then lift up the top edge and loosely fold to the middle then fold over once more – you should have something that resembles a rugby ball. Place the two loaves on a floured baking tray, cover with a tea towel and leave to rise for about 1 hour until nearly doubled in size.

8 Preheat the oven to 180°C/gas mark 4.

9 Use a sharp knife to score the top of the loaves diagonally.

10 If you have a water spray bottle, use this to spray the oven sides before placing the baking tray in the middle of the oven (this creates steam and will give colour and a nice crust to your bread – see page 15 – but don't worry if you don't have one). Bake for about 20 minutes, until the loaves are uniformly golden in colour.

STROMBOLI
Rolled focaccia stuffed with mozzarella and basil leaves

The name *stromboli* is taken from a notorious active volcano off the north coast of Sicily which is famous for its round swelling shape. This bread recipe was created around the area and is often served at weddings and birthday parties. The flavour of the melted mozzarella with the fresh basil leaves is just divine and, with the freshly grated Parmesan, makes this stuffed bread one of my favourites by far. Eat it warm to accompany a salad of your choice.

Makes 1 long loaf

350g strong white flour
plus extra for dusting

1 teaspoon salt

5g fast-action dried yeast

200ml water, warm

½ teaspoon caster sugar

2 tablespoons extra virgin olive oil
plus extra for brushing

1 tablespoon rosemary leaves

FOR THE FILLING

2 mozzarella balls, drained and cut
into little cubes

50g freshly grated Parmesan
cheese

3 tablespoons chopped basil leaves

1 teaspoon freshly ground
black pepper

1 garlic clove, peeled and crushed

1 Brush a baking tray and the inside of a large bowl with oil.

2 Mix the flour, salt, sugar and yeast into a large bowl and make a well in the centre. Pour in the water and mix until you have a sticky soft dough.

3 Transfer the dough to a lightly floured surface and knead for 10 minutes until smooth and elastic. Shape it into a ball and place in the oiled bowl. Brush the top with a little oil, cover with clingfilm and leave it to rise in a warm place away from draughts for 1 hour.

4 Transfer the dough to a lightly floured surface and roll out into a rectangle measuring about 30 x 25cm. Cover with clingfilm and leave to rest for 5 minutes.

5 Place the ingredients for the filling in a large bowl and mix to combine.

6 Scatter the filling over the rolled out dough to within 1cm of the edges.

7 Starting from the shorter side, roll up the dough like a Swiss roll, tucking the side edges under to seal. Transfer the roll, seam down, onto the oiled baking tray. Cover with clingfilm and leave to rest in a warm place away from draughts for 30 minutes.

8 Preheat the oven to 200°C/gas mark 6.

9 Brush the roll with the extra virgin olive oil and use a skewer to prick holes all over the bread. Sprinkle over the rosemary leaves.

10 Bake in the middle of the oven for 35 minutes. Remove from the oven and transfer to a wire rack to cool down.

11 Slice and serve warm with a little salad of your choice.

PAGNOTTA AI QUATTRO FORMAGGI
Four cheeses rustic loaf

The ultimate cheesy bread. For breakfast, brunch, lunch, afternoon break, dinner ... this is the one that will satisfy all your desires when it comes to flavoured bread. Eaten warm this bread is at its best, so if you are using it a day after you made it, pop in it back into the oven for a few minutes before serving. Four very different cheeses have never worked so well together before. A great bread to pack into a lunchbox with a few slices of salami or Parma ham.

Makes 1 round loaf

350g strong white flour
plus extra for dusting

100g wholewheat flour

1 teaspoon salt

2 teaspoons caster sugar

7g fast-action dried yeast

1 medium egg

180ml water, warm

100g mascarpone cheese

50g Gorgonzola cheese, cut into
1cm cubes

50g freshly grated Parmesan cheese

50g freshly grated pecorino cheese

3 tablespoons chopped
fresh chives

Olive oil for brushing

FOR THE GLAZE

1 medium egg

1 tablespoon water

Freshly ground black pepper

1 Brush a baking tray and the inside of a large bowl with oil.

2 Mix the flours, salt, sugar and yeast together in a large bowl and make a well in the centre. Pour in the water with the egg and mascarpone cheese. Mix with your fingertips until you have a soft dough.

3 Transfer the dough to a lightly floured surface and knead for 5 minutes. Fold in the Gorgonzola, Parmesan, pecorino and chives and continue to knead for a further 5 minutes. Shape it into a ball and place in the oiled bowl. Cover with clingfilm and leave to rise in a warm place away from draughts for 1 hour.

4 Turn the dough out onto a lightly floured surface and gently punch down. Transfer to the oiled baking tray and shape into a 20cm round loaf. Cover with clingfilm and leave it to rise in a warm place away from draughts for 45 minutes.

5 Preheat the oven to 200°C/gas mark 6.

6 In a small bowl, mix together the egg and water and brush over the top of the bread. Sprinkle with black pepper.

7 Use a sharp knife to score the top of the loaf into eight equal segments.

8 Bake in the middle of the oven for 35 minutes until golden all over. Transfer to a wire rack to cool.

PAGNOTTA ANTICA CON FARINA DI SEGALE

Old-fashioned rye bread

My grandfather Giovanni first showed me this recipe when I was about 8 years old and I can still remember the beautiful smell of the rye flour with the fresh honey. This is probably one of the oldest bread recipes that I know and it remains a favourite in my family. Sliced and toasted, this *pagnotta* will make the perfect bread for bruschetta or garlic bread.

Makes 1 round loaf

250g rye flour plus extra for dusting

200g strong white flour plus extra for dusting

2 teaspoons salt

10g fast-action dried yeast

150ml water, warm

130ml full-fat milk, warm

2 teaspoons clear runny honey

Olive oil for brushing

1 Brush a baking tray and the inside of a large bowl with oil.

2 Mix the flours, salt and yeast together in a large bowl and make a well in the centre. Pour in the water with the milk and honey. Mix with your fingertips until you have a soft dough.

3 Transfer the dough to a lightly floured surface and knead for 10 minutes until smooth, elastic and firm. Shape it into a ball and place in the oiled bowl. Cover with clingfilm and leave it to rise in a warm place away from draughts for 3 hours.

4 Turn out the dough onto a lightly floured surface and punch down. Shape into a round loaf and place on the oiled baking tray, dust the top with rye flour and cover with clingfilm. Leave it to rise in a warm place away from draughts for 1½ hours.

5 Preheat the oven to 220°C/gas mark 7.

6 Use a sharp knife to slash the loaf with 2 long cuts about 3cm apart.

7 Bake in the middle of the oven for 35 minutes or until the loaf sounds hollow when tapped on the base.

8 Transfer to a wire rack to cool and serve warm to accompany a platter of grilled fish or meats.

PAGNOTTA CON FINOCCHIETTO
Farmhouse loaf encrusted with fennel seeds

This basic rustic bread will surprise you with the flavour it delivers! It takes me back to my catering school days, when the smell seemed to fill the streets and my friends and I would use all our charm to persuade the baker to give us a piece or two! It is a large loaf with excellent keeping qualities, so if you are looking for a bread to last all week, this is the one for you. I have added fennel seeds, which impart a strong flavour, but you can leave it plain or substitute sesame or poppy seeds if you prefer.

Makes 1 oval loaf

450g strong white flour

1 teaspoon salt plus an extra pinch for the topping

1 tablespoon caster sugar

10g fast-action dried yeast

1 tablespoon fennel seeds, crushed

280ml water, warm

30g salted butter, melted

1 egg white

Olive oil for brushing

1   Brush a baking tray and the inside of a large bowl with oil.

2   Sift the flour into a large bowl with the salt, sugar and yeast and make a well in the centre. Sprinkle over ½ teaspoon of the fennel seeds and pour in the water with the butter. Mix with your fingertips until you have a soft dough.

3   Transfer the dough to a lightly floured surface and knead for 10 minutes until smooth and elastic. Shape it into a ball and place in the oiled bowl. Cover with clingfilm and leave it to rise in a warm place away from draughts for 1 hour.

4   Turn out the dough onto a lightly floured surface and punch down. Shape into an oval and place on the oiled baking tray. Brush the top with a little oil and cover with clingfilm. Leave it to rise in a warm place away from draughts for 40 minutes.

5   Preheat the oven to 220°C/gas mark 7.

6   In a small bowl, mix the egg white with the pinch of salt.

7   Brush the top of the loaf with the egg white and sprinkle over the remaining fennel seeds. Use a sharp knife to make a cut right down its length.

8   Bake in the middle of the oven for 20 minutes, then reduce the temperature to 180°C/gas mark 4 and continue to bake for a further 10 minutes.

9   Transfer to a wire rack to cool slightly and serve warm with your favourite selection of cured hams or salami.

PAGNOTTA LIGURE CON PATATE
Ligurian rustic loaf with potatoes and rosemary

I love potatoes and rosemary together and I thought adding it to a crusty type bread would be a surprising and exciting combination – and it really works. It's a heavy and filling bread and would be perfect with a soup or amazing with some poached or fried eggs. If you love carbs – this is the bread for you. I wouldn't suggest serving it with a starter followed by other courses, though, as it will fill up your guests too soon. This is Ligurian bread at its best. Always bake it with fresh rosemary; the dried version will be useless.

Makes 1 oval loaf

250g floury potatoes, peeled and diced

350g strong white flour plus extra for dusting

110g wholemeal flour plus extra for sprinkling

2 teaspoons salt

7g fast-action dried yeast

150ml water, warm

1 tablespoon fresh rosemary leaves, finely chopped

30g salted butter, melted

Olive oil for brushing

1 Cook the potatoes in boiling water until tender. Drain, then mash and sieve them and leave to cool.

2 Brush a baking tray and the inside of a large bowl with oil.

3 Mix the flours with the salt, rosemary and yeast in a large bowl and make a well in the centre. Pour in the water with the butter and the potatoes. Gently mix all the ingredients together until you have a soft dough.

4 Transfer the dough to a lightly floured surface and knead for 10 minutes until smooth and elastic. Shape it into a ball and place in the oiled bowl. Cover with clingfilm and leave it to rise in a warm place away from draughts for 1 hour.

5 Turn out the dough onto a lightly floured surface and punch down. Shape into an oval and place on the oiled baking tray. Brush the top with a little oil and sprinkle over some wholemeal flour. Cover with clingfilm and leave it to rise in a warm place away from draughts for 30 minutes.

6 Preheat the oven to 200°C/gas mark 6.

7 Use a sharp knife to slash the top with 4 diagonal cuts to make a criss-cross effect.

8 Bake in the middle of the oven for 30 minutes.

9 To test that the bread is cooked through, tap the bottom of the loaf – it should sound hollow.

10 Transfer to a wire rack to cool slightly and serve warm with your favourite soup.

SCHIACCIATA AL ROSMARINO
Schiacciata with fresh rosemary

A traditional Tuscan flatbread that will go fantastically with any of your starters. If you have any left over, put in an airtight container and take to the office with a few slices of ham or some roasted vegetables.

Makes 6 pieces

500g strong white flour

2 teaspoons sea salt

1 teaspoon caster sugar

5g fast-action dried yeast

2 tablespoons extra virgin olive oil plus extra for brushing

300ml water, warm

FOR THE TOPPING

3 tablespoons extra virgin olive oil

30g fresh rosemary leaves, chopped

1 teaspoon sea salt

1 Brush the inside of a large bowl with oil.

2 Sift the flour into a large bowl, add the sea salt, sugar and yeast, and mix all the ingredients together. Make a well in the centre and pour in the extra virgin olive oil and water. With the help of a wooden spoon, start mixing until all the ingredients are blended together, then transfer the mixture onto a floured surface and knead by hand for about 10 minutes until the dough is smooth and elastic.

3 Place the dough in the oiled bowl, cover with clingfilm and leave it to rise in a warm place away from draughts for about 2 hours until it is at least double in size.

4 Transfer the dough to a lightly floured surface, and divide into 6 equal pieces, forming each one into an oval shape about 15cm long. Place the pieces on 2 lightly floured baking trays and leave to rest for 20–30 minutes.

5 Taking each dough piece in turn, use your fingertips to flatten them out to a thickness of 1–1.5cm and about 20cm long and 10cm wide. Return to the baking trays, brush with extra virgin olive oil and sprinkle with the chopped rosemary and a pinch of sea salt. Use a sharp pizza cutter to make 3 diagonal cuts across the top of the *schiacciata*.

6 Cover with a tea towel and leave to rise in a warm place away from draughts for 1 hour. Preheat the oven to 180°C/gas mark 4.

7 Before baking the bread, widen the cuts with your fingertips so that once it is baked it will be easier to tear and share.

8 Bake for 12–15 minutes, or until golden brown in colour. Remove the *schiacciata* from the oven and place on a wire rack to cool slightly before serving.

SCHIACCIATA CON AGLIO E PREZZEMOLO

Schiacciata with garlic and parsley

A simple and tasty recipe suitable as an aperitif or snack, accompanied by a glass of chilled white wine.

Makes 6 pieces

500g strong white flour

2 teaspoons sea salt

1 teaspoon caster sugar

5g fast-action dried yeast

2 tablespoons extra virgin olive oil plus extra for brushing

350ml water, warm

FOR THE TOPPING

3 tablespoons extra virgin olive oil

30g freshly chopped garlic

6 teaspoons freshly chopped flatleaf parsley

1 teaspoon sea salt

1 Brush a baking tray and the inside of a large bowl with oil.

2 Sift the flour into a large bowl, add the sea salt, sugar and yeast, and mix all the ingredients together. Make a well in the centre and pour in the extra virgin olive oil and water. With the help of a wooden spoon, start mixing until all the ingredients are blended together, then transfer the mixture onto a floured surface and knead by hand for about 10 minutes until the dough is smooth and elastic.

3 Place the dough in the oiled bowl, cover with clingfilm and leave it to rise in a warm place away from draughts for about 2 hours until it is at least double in size.

4 Transfer the dough to a lightly floured surface, and divide into 6 equal pieces, forming each one into an oval shape about 15cm long. Place the pieces on 2 lightly floured baking trays and leave to rest for 20–30 minutes.

5 Taking each dough piece in turn, use your fingertips to flatten them out to a thickness of 1–1.5cm and about 20cm long and 10cm wide. Return to the baking trays, brush with extra virgin olive oil and sprinkle with the chopped garlic and parsley and a pinch of sea salt. Use a sharp pizza cutter to make 3 diagonal cuts across the top of the *schiacciata*.

6 Cover with a tea towel and leave to rise in a warm place away from draughts for 1 hour. Preheat the oven to 180°C/gas mark 4.

7 Before baking the bread, widen the cuts with your fingertips so that once it is baked it will be easier to tear and share.

8 Bake for 12–15 minutes, or until golden brown in colour. Remove the *schiacciata* from the oven and place on a wire rack to cool slightly before serving.

PANE CON SEMI DI ZUCCA E GIRASOLE

Pumpkin and sunflower seed bread

Seed breads are very popular and using seeds enhances the bread with that extra nutty flavour that we all love. The appearance of this large round loaf is great and it's also deceiving: the uncut top makes you think that you are going to enjoy a sunflower seed loaf, but once you cut into it, the pumpkin and sesame seeds surprise you. This bread is light in texture but heavy in taste – you'll love it. It also used to be my grandfather Gennaro's favourite bread ... gosh I miss him!

Makes 1 round loaf

270g strong white flour
60g fine polenta
1 teaspoon salt
10g fast-action dried yeast
100ml water, warm
140ml full-fat milk, warm
2 tablespoons pumpkin seeds
1 tablespoon sesame seeds
2 tablespoons sunflower seeds
Olive oil for brushing

1 Brush a baking tray and the inside of a large bowl with oil.

2 Mix the flours, salt and yeast together in a large bowl and make a well in the centre. Pour in the water with the milk and mix until you have a soft dough.

3 Transfer the dough to a lightly floured surface and knead for 5 minutes until smooth and elastic. Shape it into a ball and place in the oiled bowl. Cover with clingfilm and leave it to rise in a warm place away from draughts for 1 hour.

4 Turn out the dough onto a lightly floured surface and punch down. Flatten out and sprinkle over the pumpkin seeds, sesame seeds and 1 tablespoon of the sunflower seeds. Fold up and knead again for 2 minutes. Leave it to rest for 5 minutes then shape into a round ball and flatten slightly.

5 Place on the oiled baking tray, brush the top with a little oil and cover with clingfilm. Leave it to rise in a warm place away from draughts for 50 minutes.

6 Preheat the oven to 200°C/gas mark 6.

7 Brush the top of the loaf with water and evenly sprinkle over the remaining sunflower seeds. Bake in the middle of the oven for 35 minutes.

8 Transfer to a wire rack to cool slightly and serve warm or at room temperature.

PANE DELLA SICILIA
Sicilian bread with semolina and sesame seeds

A traditional Sicilian bread that is particularly light, with a thin crispy crust and springy crumb. The semolina flour gives it a warm yellowish tone and also adds a subtle sweet buttery taste. The sesame seed topping adds another dimension, so do use them if you can! Try this bread served warm with fish, grilled vegetables or a selection of your favourite cheeses.

Makes 1 loaf

450g fine semolina

120g strong white flour

2 teaspoons salt

10g fast-action dried yeast

360ml water, warm

1 tablespoon extra virgin olive oil plus extra for brushing

1 tablespoon walnut or sesame seed oil

Sesame seeds for decoration

1   Brush a baking tray and the inside of a large bowl with oil.

2   Sift the semolina and flour into a large bowl, add the salt and yeast, and mix together. Make a well in the centre, pour in the water with the oils and gradually incorporate all the ingredients to create a firm dough.

3   Turn out the dough onto a lightly floured surface and knead for 10 minutes until smooth and elastic. Shape into a ball and place in the oiled bowl. Cover with clingfilm and leave to rise in a warm place away from draughts for 1½ hours.

4   Turn out the dough onto a lightly floured surface and punch down. Knead gently for 30 seconds and then shape into a fat roll about 50cm long. Form the roll into an 'S' shape (to symbolise the first letter of the word Sicily).

5   Carefully transfer the 'S' shape to the oiled baking tray and brush the top with a little oil. Cover with clingfilm and leave it to rise in a warm place away from draughts for 35 minutes.

6   Preheat the oven to 220°C/gas mark 7.

7   Brush the top of the loaf with water and sprinkle over the sesame seeds. Spray the inside of the oven with water and bake the loaf for 10 minutes.

8   Reduce the oven temperature to 200°C/gas mark 6 and continue to cook for a further 30 minutes until beautiful and golden.

9   Transfer to a wire rack to cool slightly and serve warm.

PANE PIATTO ALL'ORZO E LIMONE
Barley flatbread with lemon zest

If you are looking for a light bread for starter or dips this is the one to choose. The cream, milk and butter create a lovely soft smooth texture but the kick of the lemon means the bread is light and fresh. If you prefer, though, you can substitute the lemon zest with orange zest. Most breads are lovely either warm or cold but this one is definitely best served at room temperature – *fantastico* with dips or cottage cheese.

Makes 1 small round flatbread

230g barley flour
1 teaspoon salt
2 teaspoons baking powder
30g salted butter, melted
120ml single cream
4 tablespoons full-fat milk
Zest of 1 unwaxed lemon
Olive oil for brushing

1 Brush a baking tray with oil and preheat the oven to 200°C/gas mark 6.

2 Sift the flour, salt and baking powder into a large bowl. Pour in the butter, cream, milk and lastly add the lemon zest. Mix all the ingredients together to create a dough.

3 Turn out the dough onto a lightly floured surface and shape into a flat round shape about 1cm thick.

4 Transfer to the baking tray and with use a sharp knife to lightly score the top into 8 sections.

5 Prick the top evenly with a fork and bake in the middle of the oven for 18 minutes.

6 Serve and enjoy.

PIADINE ROMAGNOLE
Flatbread flavoured with oregano

A traditional Roman peasant bread at its best. Its humble origins don't do it justice, as it is has long been an essential part of the Romans' diet, evolved and adapted over the years to become a firm favourite with country folk. *Piadine* is a robust and versatile bread, suitable for almost any occasion. Crusty but with an open, airy interior, this is really an 'anything goes' bread. *Fantastico* to use when serving dips to your friends and family.

Makes 4 flatbreads

180g strong white flour plus extra for dusting

1 teaspoon dried oregano

1 teaspoon salt

1 tablespoon extra virgin olive oil plus extra for brushing

110ml water, warm

1 Brush the inside of a large bowl with oil.

2 Sift the flour in a large bowl; add in the oregano and the salt. Make a well in the centre and pour in the oil with the water. Mix all the ingredients together to form a dough.

3 Transfer the dough to a lightly floured surface and knead for 5 minutes until smooth and elastic. Place in the oiled bowl, cover with clingfilm and leave to rest in a warm place away from draughts for 20 minutes.

4 Divide the dough into 4 equal pieces and roll each one into an 18cm disc. Cover with a tea towel until ready to cook.

5 Lightly oil a large frying pan and place over a medium heat.

6 Cook each disc for 2 minutes on each side until they are starting to brown all over.

7 Serve the *piadine* warm to accompany your favourite soup or dips.

CIABATTINE SCHIACCIATE CON AGLIO E PREZZEMOLO

Flat ciabatta with fresh garlic and parsley

The perfect party bread. I often make my *ciabattine* when the boys are coming round for a game of pool or to watch football. I have tried making them using powdered garlic, but it doesn't work as well as a fresh clove. Serve the *ciabattine* warm to accompany a good hummus or with a few good-quality marinated olives.

Makes 8

250g self-raising flour
½ teaspoon salt
½ teaspoon ground white pepper
3 tablespoons plain 'live' yogurt
Plain flour for dusting

FOR THE TOPPING

1 garlic clove, peeled and crushed
2 tablespoons freshly chopped
 flatleaf parsley
50g salted butter, melted

1 Sift the flour, salt and pepper into a large bowl. Pour in the yogurt and water, a little at a time, working the ingredients together with your fingers. Create a soft, slightly sticky dough, cover with clingfilm and leave for 1 hour to ferment in a warm place. (Please remember that the dough will not rise as it's a yeast-free mixture.)

2 Heat the grill with a wire grill rack to its highest setting.

3 Mix the garlic and parsley with the melted butter and set aside.

4 Transfer the dough to a lightly floured surface and divide equally into 8 balls. Pressing down with your fingertips, form each ball into a flat oval shape about 20cm long.

5 Cook the flat breads in batches under the hot grill for 1½ minutes on each side until golden and puffed up.

6 Brush one side of the bread with the flavoured butter and serve warm to accompany dips or antipasti.

FILONCINO SCHIACCIATO CON OLIVE E TIMO

Flat baguette with green olives and thyme

This bread from Campagna is the Italian cousin of France's long and airy baguette. Serve with your favourite extra virgin olive oil and balsamic vinegar for dipping.

Makes 6 pieces

500g strong white flour
10g salt
1 teaspoon caster sugar
5g fast-action dried yeast
2 tablespoons extra virgin olive oil
350ml water

FOR THE TOPPING

3 tablespoons extra virgin olive oil
120g pitted green olive
2 tablespoons finely chopped fresh
   thyme leaves

1 Brush the inside of a large bowl with oil.

2 Sift the flour into a large bowl, add the salt, sugar and yeast and mix the dry ingredients together. Make a well in the centre and pour in the extra virgin olive oil and water. With the help of a wooden spoon, start mixing until all the ingredients are blended together then transfer the mixture onto a floured surface and knead by hand for about 10 minutes until the dough is smooth and elastic.

3 Place the dough in the oiled bowl, cover with clingfilm and leave to rise in a warm place away from draughts for about 1–1½ hours until it has at least doubled in size.

4 Divide the dough into 6 equal pieces, and work each one on a floured work surface, shaping them into batons about 20cm long. Place them on a floured baking tray to rest for 10–15 minutes.

5 Taking each piece in turn, stretch the batons to about 30cm in length then use your fingertips to flatten them out to a thickness of 1–1.5cm. Return the batons to the baking tray, brush with extra virgin olive oil, top each one with a few of the whole pitted olives and sprinkle with thyme. Cover with a tea towel and leave to rise in a warm place away from draughts for 1 hour. Preheat the oven to 180°C/gas mark 4.

6 Place the baking tray in the middle of the oven and bake the *filoncino* for 12–15 minutes, until they are golden brown in colour. Remove from the oven and serve.

PANINI ALL'OLIO

Soft bread rolls enriched with extra virgin olive oil

Panini translates simply as 'roll' in Italian, designed specifically as a handy carrier for a sandwich filling. Toasted, the panini takes on another dimension; all the flavours are enhanced, you can taste the fruitiness of the olive oil in the dough, the filling often oozes out alluringly, and the crust becomes deliciously crispy, while the centre melts in the mouth. Irresistible!

Makes 12 rolls

500g strong white flour
1 teaspoon sea salt
7g fast-action dried yeast
180ml fresh milk
70ml extra virgin olive oil
100ml water

1　Brush the inside of a large bowl with oil.

2　Sift the flour into a large bowl. Make a well in the centre and add the salt, yeast, fresh milk, extra virgin olive oil and water. With the help of a wooden spoon, start mixing until all the ingredients are blended together then transfer the mixture onto a floured surface and finish kneading by hand for about 10–15 minutes. Knead the dough until it becomes smooth and silky (the dough may seem quite sticky but this is what gives the panini a lighter, fluffier texture).

3　Place the dough in the oiled bowl, cover with clingfilm and leave to rise in a warm place away from draughts for about 1–1½ hours until it has at least doubled in size.

4　Divide the dough into 12 equal pieces, and work each one on a floured work surface, aiming for regular round-shaped rolls. Line up the bread rolls on a floured baking tray (make sure that they are spaced well apart – use a second tray if needed), cover with a tea towel and leave to rise in a warm place away from draughts for 45 minutes or until doubled in size. Preheat the oven to 180°C/gas mark 4.

5　Place the baking tray in the middle of the oven and bake for about 10 minutes, until the panini are uniformly golden in colour.

6　Serve warm, filled with ham or cheese.

PANINI DA COLAZIONE
Breakfast rolls

I know that this recipe is entitled 'Breakfast Rolls' but believe me, filled with my suggested bacon and fried egg, you would be happy to have one of these handed to you at almost any time of day. These rolls are light in texture and yet very flavoursome and actually work well with a savoury or sweet filling. If you start the day with one (maybe two) of my breakfast rolls, I promise you will definitely have a great day.

Makes 10 rolls

450g plain flour plus extra
    for dusting

2 teaspoons salt

10g fast-action dried yeast

150ml full-fat milk, warm,
    plus extra for glazing

150ml water, warm

Olive oil for brushing

1. Brush 2 baking trays with oil.

2. Sift the flour into a large bowl, mix in the salt and yeast and make a well in the centre. Pour in the milk and water and combine all the ingredients to form a soft dough.

3. Lightly knead the dough in the bowl, cover with clingfilm and leave it to rise in a warm place away from draughts for 1 hour.

4. Turn out the dough onto a lightly floured surface and punch down. Divide into 10 equal pieces, knead each one lightly then shape into balls. Use a rolling pin to make flat rounds about 9cm diameter.

5. Transfer the rolls onto the oiled baking trays (make sure that they are spaced well apart) and cover with clingfilm. Leave to rise in a warm place away from draughts for 30 minutes.

6. Preheat the oven to 200°C/gas mark 6.

7. With your fingers, gently press the centre of each roll to even out the air bubbles (this will also prevent the rolls from blistering). Glaze the tops with milk and dust with flour.

8. Place the baking trays in the middle of the oven and bake for 18 minutes. Remove, dust with more flour and leave to cool on a wire rack.

9. Serve the panini warm, each filled with crispy bacon and a fried egg.

PANINI AL GORGONZOLA
Gorgonzola and walnut rolls

There is nothing better than a strong Italian cheese with warm crusty bread – or is there? For me Gorgonzola and walnut is the ultimate combination: the flavours are incredible. You can substitute any other blue cheese and if you prefer a milder flavour use dolcelatte. Great little rolls to take to work.

Makes 12 rolls

350g strong white flour plus extra
   for dusting
350g wholemeal flour
7g fast-action dried yeast
1 teaspoon salt
200ml full-fat milk, warm
250ml water, warm
180g Gorgonzola cheese, cubed
90g walnuts, roughly chopped
Olive oil for brushing

1   Brush 2 baking trays with oil.

2   Combine the flours, yeast and salt together into a large bowl and make a well in the centre. Pour in the milk with the water and mix all the ingredients to form a soft dough.

3   Turn out the dough onto a lightly floured surface and knead for 10 minutes. Gently work in the Gorgonzola and walnuts. Return the dough to the bowl, brush the top with a little oil and cover with clingfilm. Leave to rise in a warm place away from draughts for 1 hour.

4   Turn out the dough onto a lightly floured surface. Divide the dough into 12 equal pieces and shape into balls. Arrange the balls on the prepared baking trays (make sure that they are spaced well apart – use a second tray if needed) and cover with clingfilm. Leave to rise in a warm place away from draughts for 45 minutes.

5   Preheat the oven to 220°C/gas mark 7.

6   Remove the clingfilm and bake in the middle of the oven for 20 minutes until golden brown. Remove from the trays and leave to cool slightly on a wire rack.

7   Serve the rolls warm or take them on your next picnic.

PANINI IMBOTTITI DI FORMAGGIO
Stuffed buns with oozing Taleggio and Cheddar cheese

Taleggio is the perfect cheese for stuffing. Its oozing quality is excellent and the flavour, paired with Cheddar, works brilliantly in this bread. If you are looking for a stronger combination, use Stinking Bishop instead of Taleggio. This is definitely a different way to use a Yorkshire pudding tin. *Buon Appetito!*

Makes 4 buns

230g plain strong flour plus extra for dusting

1 teaspoon salt

7g fast-action dried yeast

150ml full-fat milk, warm

25g salted butter, at room temperature

Olive oil for brushing

FOR THE FILLING

250g Taleggio cheese, cut into 1cm cubes

200g grated Cheddar cheese

1 medium egg, lightly beaten

1 tablespoon salted butter, at room temperature

½ teaspoon paprika

FOR THE GLAZE

1 egg yolk plus 1 tablespoon water, mixed together

1   Brush a four-hole/10cm diameter Yorkshire pudding tin with oil. Brush the inside of a large bowl with oil.

2   Mix the flour, salt and yeast into a large bowl and make a well in the centre. Pour in the milk and mix to form a dough. Transfer onto a lightly floured surface and knead in the butter for 5 minutes until you have a smooth and elastic dough. Place the dough into a lightly oiled bowl and cover with clingfilm. Leave to rise in a warm place away from draughts for 1½ hours.

3   Meanwhile place the cheeses in a large bowl with the egg, butter and paprika. Stir all the ingredients together and set aside.

4   Turn the dough out onto a lightly floured surface and knead for 3 minutes. Divide into 4 pieces and roll each one into a 18cm disc.

5   Place 1 disc in one of the Yorkshire pudding tin holes and fill with a quarter of the cheese mixture. Gather the overhanging dough into the centre and twist to form a topknot. Repeat the process with the remaining discs and filling.

6   Brush the top of the filled panini with a little oil and cover with clingfilm. Leave to rise in a warm place away from draughts for 30 minutes.

7   Preheat the oven to 180°C/gas mark 4.

8   Brush the top of the panini with the prepared glaze and bake in the middle of the oven for 28 minutes.

9   Leave the panini to cool in the pudding tin for 3 minutes then turn out onto a wire rack.

10 Serve warm with a cold beer. For the following day, these make great little buns for a packed lunch.

PIEGATA AL PESTO VERDE
Folded bread with basil pesto

A fantastic Italian bread to enjoy as a snack or take on a picnic. If you prefer you can substitute the green pesto with sun-dried tomato paste. For the best flavour, eat it warm.

Makes 4 pieces

500g strong white flour

2 teaspoons sea salt

1 teaspoon caster sugar

5g fast-action dried yeast

2 tablespoons extra virgin olive oil

300ml water, warm

FOR THE FILLING

4 tablespoons good-quality
   basil pesto

4 teaspoons freshly grated
   Parmesan cheese

1   Brush the inside of a large bowl with oil.

2   Sift the flour into a large bowl and add the sea salt, sugar and yeast, and mix all the ingredients together. Make a well in the centre and pour in the olive oil and water. With the help of a wooden spoon start mixing until all the ingredients are blended together, then transfer the mixture onto a floured surface and knead by hand for about 10 minutes until the dough is smooth and elastic.

3   Place the dough in the oiled bowl, cover with clingfilm and leave to rise in a warm place away from draughts for about 2 hours until it has at least doubled in size.

4   When the dough is well risen, divide into 4 equal pieces and shape into round balls. Leave to rest for a further 20 minutes on a lightly floured surface. Then, with your fingertips, gently start to press the dough out, extending each piece to form a rough circle about 2cm thick. Place on a floured baking tray.

5   Spread each dough circle with 1 tablespoon of pesto and sprinkle with 1 teaspoon of Parmesan. Then take the edge of the dough and fold over loosely to form a half-moon shape. Pull the ends just to extend it slightly (the dough does not need to be sealed). Leave to rise for a further 40 minutes.

6   Preheat the oven to 180°C/gas mark 4.

7   Bake in the middle of the oven for 15–20 minutes until the bread is golden brown. Remove from the oven and serve.

TASCA RIPIENA
Rolled bread with cheese and ham

These can be served simply on their own as a starter, straight from the oven. Delicious!

Makes 8 pieces

500g strong white flour
2 teaspoons sea salt
1 teaspoon caster sugar
5g fast-action dried yeast
2 tablespoons extra virgin olive oil
300ml water, warm

FOR THE FILLING

60g sliced ham
100g Emmental cheese cut into
  1cm cubes

1 Brush the inside of a large bowl with oil.

2 Sift the flour into a large bowl and add the sea salt, sugar and yeast, and mix all the ingredients together. Make a well in the centre and pour in the olive oil and water. With the help of a wooden spoon start mixing until all the ingredients are blended together, then transfer the mixture onto a floured surface and knead by hand for about 10 minutes until the dough is smooth and elastic.

3 Place the dough in the oiled bowl, cover with clingfilm and leave to rise in a warm place away from draughts for 1–1½ hours until it has at least doubled in size.

4 When the dough is well risen divide into 8 equal pieces and shape into round balls. Leave to rest for a further 10 minutes on a lightly floured surface. Then, with a rolling pin, roll out each piece until 1–2cm thick and scatter over the sliced ham and cubed Emmental.

5 Roll up the dough Swiss-roll fashion to form a stick about 18cm long then use your hands to gently roll the stick slightly to seal the dough. At this point you should have a 25cm long roll. Continue to make 8 sticks then transfer them to 2 floured baking trays (seam-side down to prevent the cheese oozing out) and leave to rise for a further 40 minutes. Use a sharp knife to make 3 oblique cuts on the top of the sticks.

6 Preheat the oven to 180°C/gas mark 4.

7 Bake in the middle of the oven for 15–20 minutes until the bread is golden brown. Remove from the oven and serve.

PANINI LUNGHI AL PEPE NERO
Long panini with black pepper topping

Panini translates simply as 'roll' in Italian but the word has become widely recognised in the UK as a rectangular soft roll with grill marks, designed specifically as a handy carrier for sandwich fillings before being grilled as a toasty snack. This panini recipe is special, its pepper crust gives a great kick but the interior remains light and airy. It makes the perfect versatile sandwich base – a blank canvas for any number of favourite combos. Simply delicious served warm!

Makes 6 panini

230g strong white flour plus
   extra for dusting

7g fast-action dried yeast

1 teaspoon salt

140ml water, warm

Extra virgin olive oil for brushing

Freshly ground black pepper

1   Brush the inside of a large bowl with oil.

2   Sift the flour into a large bowl, stir in the yeast and salt and make a well in the centre. Pour in the water and mix to form a soft dough.

3   Turn out the dough onto a lightly floured surface and knead for 10 minutes until smooth and elastic. Place in the oiled bowl, cover with clingfilm and leave to rest in a warm place away from draughts for 50 minutes.

4   Turn out the dough onto a lightly floured surface and punch down. Divide into 6 equal pieces and roll out each one to make a rectangle measuring about 10 x 5cm and 1cm thick.

5   Transfer the panini to 2 floured baking trays (make sure that they are spaced well apart) and use a sharp knife to make 4 slashes on top of each one. Brush the top with a little oil and cover with clingfilm. Leave to rise in a warm place away from draughts for 20 minutes.

6   Preheat the oven to 200°C/gas mark 6.

7   Brush the tops with more oil and sprinkle with ground black pepper all over.

8   Place the trays in the middle of the oven and bake for 15 minutes.

9   Remove and transfer the panini to a wire rack to cool slightly. Serve warm or at room temperature.

PIEGATA CON POMODORINI
Folded bread with semi-dried tomatoes

A traditional northern Italian folded bread, often used to accompany starters or an aperitif. You can of course try it with green basil pesto instead of the red one or even with an olive tapenade. Ensure that you use a strong white flour and please, please, please, a good-quality extra virgin olive oil. This is the best folded bread you will ever experience!

Makes 4 pieces

500g strong white flour plus
    extra for dusting

1 teaspoon salt

1 teaspoon caster sugar

7g fast-action dried yeast

3 tablespoons extra virgin olive oil
    plus extra for brushing

300ml water, warm

FOR THE FILLING

80g red pesto

150g semi-dried tomatoes in oil,
    drained

4 teaspoons freshly grated
    Parmesan cheese

1   Brush a large baking tray with oil.

2   Mix the flour, salt, sugar and yeast in a large bowl and make a well in the centre. Pour in the oil and water and mix all the ingredients together to form a dough.

3   Transfer the dough to a lightly floured surface and knead for 10 minutes until smooth and elastic. Shape it into a ball and put back into the bowl. Brush the top with a little oil, cover with clingfilm and leave it to rise in a warm place away from draughts for 1 hour.

4   Turn out the dough onto a lightly floured surface and divide into 4 equal pieces. Cover with clingfilm and leave to rest in a warm place away from draughts for 30 minutes.

5   Transfer the pieces to the oiled baking tray and with your fingertips, gently press down each piece to form a disc about 2cm thick.

6   Spread the pesto over the 4 discs and scatter the semi-dried tomatoes on top. Sprinkle with Parmesan and fold the discs to form half-moon shapes. Do be sure *not* to seal the edges.

7   Cover the folded bread with clingfilm and leave to rest in a warm place away from draughts for 45 minutes.

8   Preheat the oven to 180°C/gas mark 4.

9   Bake in the middle of the oven for 18 minutes. Remove and transfer the *piegata* to a wire rack to cool slightly and serve warm.

SCHIACCIATINE ROTONDE CON MENTA E CIPOLLE

Round flat rolls with fresh mint and onion topping

Any onion bread is tasty but you just have to try this one ... the combination of onion and fresh mint is amazing. It is a perfect bread to serve with antipasti – especially if you have many starter dishes with lots of different flavours. You can substitute the fresh mint with fresh rosemary leaves but, if you ask me, mint works brilliantly. My mother use to give me and my sister Marcella this *schiacciatine* for our school packed lunch. Delicious with a little soft cheese on the side!

Makes 8 rolls

450g strong white flour plus extra
    for dusting
1 teaspoon salt
10g fast-action dried yeast
280ml water, warm
1 small white onion, finely chopped
2 teaspoons ground coriander
1 tablespoon freshly chopped
    mint leaves
½ teaspoon freshly ground
    black pepper
Extra virgin olive oil for brushing

1   Brush the inside of a large bowl with oil.

2   Mix the flour, salt, and yeast in a large bowl and and make a well in the centre. Pour in the water and mix all the ingredients together to form a firm dough.

3   Transfer the dough to a lightly floured surface and knead for 10 minutes until smooth and elastic. Place in the oiled bowl, cover with clingfilm and leave to rest in a warm place away from draughts for 1 hour.

4   Turn out the dough onto a lightly floured surface and punch down.

5   Divide the dough into 8 equal pieces and roll each one into a 15cm disc. Prick all over the top with a fork and place on 2 floured baking trays spaced well apart. Brush the tops with a little oil, cover with clingfilm and leave to rise in a warm place away from draughts for 20 minutes.

6   Preheat the oven to 200°C/gas mark 6.

7   Place the chopped onions in a medium bowl with the coriander, mint and black pepper. Mix all the ingredients together.

8   Brush the top of the rolls with a little more oil and evenly sprinkle over the onion and mint mixture.

9   Bake in the middle of the oven for 18 minutes until golden. Remove and transfer the rolls to a wire rack to cool slightly.

10   Serve the *schiacciatine* warm to accompany an antipasti platter.

ROTOLO DI VERDURE E RICOTTA
Roasted vegetable and ricotta rolls

As you probably know by now, I like to be a bit different and have often served these amazing vegetable rolls at a dinner party to accompany a starter rather than the more traditional plainer breads. These rolls are so moist and full of flavour that many a time, I double the quantities so I can have them as a packed lunch the next day. This recipe is also a great way of getting vegetables into your children and a fantastic one for your next picnic. Use rosemary instead of thyme leaves if you prefer.

Makes 8 rolls

500g strong white flour plus extra
   for dusting
2 teaspoons salt
7g fast-action dried yeast
350ml water, warm
Olive oil for brushing

FOR THE FILLING
1 medium aubergine
1 medium courgette
1 red onion
1 yellow pepper
4 tablespoons olive oil
1 tablespoon thyme leaves
250g ricotta cheese
Salt and pepper to taste

1 Brush a baking tray with oil and preheat the oven to 200°C/gas mark 6.

2 Mix the flour, salt and yeast in a large bowl and make a well in the centre. Pour in the water and mix until you have a sticky soft dough.

3 Transfer the dough to a lightly floured surface and knead for 10 minutes until smooth and elastic. Shape it into a ball and put it back in the bowl. Brush the top with a little oil, cover with clingfilm and leave it to rise in a warm place away from draughts for 1 hour.

4 Cut the aubergine, courgette, onion and pepper into 1cm cubes and place into a large ovenproof dish. Pour over the oil, add the thyme, season with salt and pepper and mix all the ingredients together. Cook in the middle of the oven for 25 minutes. Stir occasionally during this time then remove the dish and leave to cool.

5 Place the roasted vegetables in a large bowl and fold in the ricotta cheese. Set aside.

6 Transfer the dough to a lightly floured surface and roll out into a 1cm thick rectangle.

7 Spread the vegetable mixture over the dough and roll it up into a log shape. Make sure that the log is well sealed. Use a sharp knife to cut the log into 8 rolls.

8 Place the rolls onto the oiled baking tray, spaced well apart. Cover with clingfilm and leave to rest for 40 minutes in a warm place away from draughts.

9 Bake the rolls in the middle of the oven for 18–20 minutes until golden and beautiful all over.

10 Try my rolls for your children's lunchboxes or for your next picnic in the park.

PIZZICOTTI
Sweet soft butter rolls

This sweet bread comes from my home town Torre del Greco, and it's simply made with eggs, milk, butter and sugar which create a very light creamy roll. You can dredge *pizzicotti* heavily with icing sugar and serve them as sweet bread with a cup of tea. You can also fill them with cream cheese or they are perfect in the morning with your favourite jam or chocolate spread. Equally delicious just as they are, and that's the way I tend to eat them.

Makes 16 rolls

450g strong white flour
1 teaspoon salt
60g caster sugar
10g fast-action dried yeast
150g salted butter, melted, plus
  extra for brushing
120ml full-fat milk, warm
3 medium eggs, lightly beaten
Icing sugar for dusting

1   Brush a 26cm round or square loose-based cake tin with melted butter.

2   Mix the flour, salt, sugar and yeast in a large bowl and make a well in the centre. Pour in 50g of the melted butter with the milk and mix all the ingredients together. Cover the bowl with clingfilm and leave to rest at room temperature for 30 minutes.

3   Gradually work in the eggs for 10 minutes to form a soft, smooth dough. Brush the top with melted butter, cover with clingfilm and leave to rise in a warm place away from draughts for 1½ hours.

4   Turn out the dough onto a lightly floured surface and punch down. Divide into 16 equal pieces and shape into balls. Roll the balls in the remaining melted butter and place in the cake tin, spaced slightly apart. Cover with clingfilm and leave it to rise for 1 hour in a warm place away from draughts.

5   Preheat the oven to 190°C/gas mark 5.

6   Gently brush the top of the rolls with any remaining butter and bake in the middle of the oven for 25 minutes until beautiful and golden.

7   Turn out to a wire rack to cool and serve warm or at room temperature dredged with icing sugar all over.

LUMACHINE DOLCI
Sweet snail-shaped rolls

I first learned this recipe when I was 13 years old and entered the catering college in Naples. It holds lots of good memories and often I try to get my boys to cook it with me. You can add in dried fruit such as raisins or cranberries if you fancy a fruitier bread. Children will enjoy making such lovely shaped rolls so, no excuses, get baking!

Makes 16 rolls

1 medium egg

2 tablespoons sunflower oil plus extra for brushing

230g strong white flour, plus extra for dusting

½ teaspoon salt

25g caster sugar

14g fast-action dried yeast

75ml full-fat milk, warm

50g salted butter, melted

Icing sugar for dusting

1 Brush 2 baking trays and the inside of a large bowl with oil.

2 Lightly beat the egg with the oil in a small bowl.

3 Mix the flour, salt, sugar and yeast in a large bowl. Make a well in the centre and pour in the milk with the egg mixture. Mix all the ingredients together with your fingertips to form a smooth dough.

4 Turn out the dough onto a lightly floured surface and knead for 10 minutes until smooth and elastic. Place in the oiled bowl, cover with clingfilm and leave to rest in a warm place away from draughts for 1 hour.

5 Turn out the dough onto a lightly floured surface and punch down.

6 Divide the dough into 16 equal pieces and shape each one into a 35cm-long thin rope. Pour the melted butter onto a large flat plate and gently dip in the ropes.

7 Transfer each rope onto the prepared baking trays and curl into a loose spiral. Ensure that you leave 10cm space between them as they will expand. Tuck the ends under to seal. Cover with clingfilm and leave to rise in a warm place away from draughts for 45 minutes.

8 Preheat the oven to 190°C/gas mark 5.

9 Brush the rolls with a little water and dust with icing sugar.

10 Bake in the middle of the oven for 20 minutes until golden.

11 Turn out and cool on a wire rack and dust with more icing sugar to decorate.

12 Enjoy my sweet rolls warm, served with jam or marmalade.

PANINI AL LATTE
Milk bread rolls

An original Italian recipe: these small tender rolls are wonderfully soft and being crustless they are a perfect for children's lunchboxes or family picnics. My boys love them! The dough is enriched with milk, eggs and butter and a hint of sugar, all contributing towards a creamy flavour, while the texture remains incredibly light. So easy to eat, they literally melt away in the mouth! You can play around with the recipe, adding toppings such as black sesame seeds or poppy seeds to give a different finish.

Makes 8 bread rolls

15g fresh yeast (or 7g fast-action dried yeast)

250ml milk, warm

500g strong white flour

50g caster sugar (or, for a savoury version, use 10g only)

1½ teaspoons salt

100g unsalted butter, softened

1 medium egg, beaten

1 Line a baking sheet with baking parchment and dust lightly with flour.

2 In a large bowl, dissolve the yeast in 3 tablespoons of warm milk. Add 30g of flour, and 1 teaspoon of sugar. Mix and knead until you have a small dough of even consistency. Place the dough in a floured bowl, cut a cross on the top and let it stand in a warm place for 30 minutes.

3 Meanwhile, sift the remaining flour onto the work surface; add the salt and the remaining milk. At room temperature, incorporate the dough prepared earlier to this mix; add the soft butter in small pieces and remaining sugar. Knead vigorously until it starts to come away from your hands and the work surface more easily.

4 Shape the dough into a ball and put into a floured bowl (previously washed with hot water and dried), cut a cross on the top and let it rest in a warm place covered with a tea towel, for 2–2½ hours, until doubled in volume.

5 Divide the dough into 8 pieces and work each of these on a floured work surface, aiming to produce regular smooth balls. Line up the panini on the prepared baking sheet. Cover with a tea towel and leave to rise again for 30 minutes.

6 Preheat the oven to 220°C/gas mark 7.

7 Brush the surface of each roll with beaten egg (this will give them a lovely sheen). Bake in the middle of the oven for 20 minutes, until the panini are beautiful and golden. Remove and leave to cool.

SFORMATO DI ZUCCA E NOCI
Pumpkin and walnut bread

This loaf has to be served with a cheese platter. The walnuts in the soft creamy dough texture is so tasty and served with ANY cheese (my choice – a Taleggio) is just to die for. If ever I have a cheese platter, this bread is an option alongside the crackers and biscuits: do try it, you will not be disappointed! You can omit the pumpkin seeds if you prefer but please keep in the walnuts – it really does make all the difference.

Makes 1 loaf

500g pumpkin (unprepared weight)

50g salted butter, melted, plus extra for greasing

60g caster sugar

½ teaspoon grated nutmeg

3 medium eggs, lightly beaten

350g strong white flour

2 teaspoons baking powder

½ teaspoon salt

100g walnuts, roughly chopped

1 Peel the pumpkin and discard the seeds. Cut the flesh into small chunks and place in a medium saucepan. Cover with water and bring to the boil. Put the lid on, lower the heat and simmer for 25 minutes. Drain well and blitz in a food processor until you have a smooth purée. Leave to cool.

2 Grease a 22 x 11cm loaf tin with a little butter. Line the base and sides of the tin with greaseproof paper.

3 Preheat the oven to 180°C/gas mark 4.

4 Weigh 280g of the pumpkin purée and place into a large bowl. Add the butter, sugar, nutmeg and eggs and mix all the ingredients together.

5 Sift the flour, baking powder and salt into a second large bowl and make a well in the centre.

6 Pour the pumpkin mixture into the well and with the help of a wooden spoon, stir all together until smooth. Finally fold in the walnuts.

7 Pour the mixture into the prepared loaf tin and bake in the middle of the oven for 1 hour. Once cooked and golden the loaf will shrink from the sides of the tin.

8 Allow the loaf to rest for 3 minutes out of the oven before turning it out onto a wire rack to cool.

9 Serve this delicious bread with your favourite cheeses.

CAKES

CROSTATA FACILE DI ALBICOCCHE
Easy apricot and kirsch flan

Apricots aren't often used as much as I would like, yet they are are amazingly tasty and don't contain lots of water, so they are the perfect fruit to bake with. I have created the ultimate apricot flan: so far, all who have tasted it always go for a second slice. It really is easy: for this dessert canned apricots are simply better than fresh ones as they are infinitely sweeter. What's more, this delicious flan can be served warm or at room temperature, so you can make it in advance. Substitute almonds for the hazelnuts if you prefer.

Serves 8

120g filo pastry

20g salted butter, melted

120g salted butter plus extra for greasing

115g caster sugar

2 medium eggs, beaten

100g finely ground hazelnuts

50g plain flour

2 tablespoons kirsch

400g canned apricot halves, drained

2 tablespoons apricot jam

Icing sugar for dusting

1   Grease a 25cm loose-based flan tin with butter and preheat the oven to 220°C/gas mark 7.

2   Cut the filo pastry into 20cm squares and lightly brush each one with the melted butter. Line the base and sides of the flan tin with the filo squares, ensuring that each one overlaps the next. Fold in any uneven edges.

3   Cream the butter and sugar in a large bowl until pale and fluffy. Gradually whisk in the eggs. Add the hazelnuts, flour and kirsch and gently fold everything together. Spread the mixture evenly in the prepared pastry case.

4   Arrange the apricot halves on top of the mixture, placing the fruit rounded side up.

5   Put the flan tin on a baking tray and bake in the middle of the oven for 8 minutes. Reduce the heat to 190°C/gas mark 5 and continue to bake for a further 25 minutes until the filling is golden brown and firm to the touch.

6   Meanwhile, heat the apricot jam over a low heat in a small saucepan.

7   Remove the flan from the oven and brush the jam over the top.

8   Leave the flan to cool in the tin for 15 minutes before removing the outer ring and place on a wire rack to cool.

9   Dust with a little icing sugar and serve warm, or leave to cool to room temperature.

PANETTONE CLASSICO
Italian Christmas cake with dried fruits

This recipe brings back such happy memories as it's usually eaten at Christmas time. In Italy you can buy panettone all year round but it's harder to find in Britain. I had to put it in this book as it's definitely a cake that is too good to be eaten only once a year, so do try to track down a supplier. You can substitute chocolate chips for the dried fruit if you wish and if you have any leftovers, try using it to make my Panettone and Butter Pudding (see page 104). Remember, a panettone is not just for Christmas!

Serves 6

15g fresh yeast

125ml full-fat milk, warm

400g strong white flour plus extra
  for dusting

3 pinches of salt

16g fresh yeast

125ml full-fat milk, warm

2 medium eggs

80g caster sugar

2 egg yolks

150g salted butter, at room
  temperature, plus extra for
  brushing

120g mixed candied peel, chopped

60g raisins

1 Brush a 15cm diameter cake tin or soufflé dish with a little butter then line with a double layer of greaseproof paper and ensure that you leave a 'collar' of paper 8cm above the top of the tin. Oil the inside of a large bowl.

2 Melt the yeast in the milk, making sure that it is completely dissolved.

3 Setting aside 2 tablespoons of the flour, sift the remaining amount into a large bowl, sprinkle over the salt and make a well in the centre. Pour in the yeast and milk with the whole eggs and gently mix all the ingredients together to make a thick batter. Sprinkle over the reserved flour and leave the sponge in a warm place for 35 minutes.

4 Add in the sugar and egg yolks and mix together to create soft dough. Work in the soft butter then turn out onto a lightly floured surface. Knead for 5 minutes until smooth and elastic and shape into a ball.

5 Place the dough ball in the oiled bowl and cover with clingfilm. Leave it to rise in a warm place away from draughts for 2 hours.

6 Turn out the dough onto a lightly floured surface and punch down. Gently knead in the candied peel and raisins. Shape again into a ball and place in the prepared tin. Cover with clingfilm and leave it to rise in a warm place away from draughts for 1 hour.

7 Preheat the oven to 190°C/gas mark 5.

8 Use a sharp knife to cut a cross on the top and brush with a little butter.

9 Bake in the middle of the oven for 20 minutes. Lower the temperature to 180°C/gas mark 4, brush the top with more butter and continue to cook for a further 30 minutes.

10 Once out of the oven, cool the cake in the tin for 10 minutes then turn out onto a wire rack to cool.

11 Panettone is perfect served at room temperature with a cup of tea.

BUDINO DI PANETTONE
Panettone and butter pudding

By far my favourite hot pudding ever! Of course bread and butter pud ingeniously originated in Britain but it is slightly perfected by the panettone. If you prefer, you can substitute Grand Marnier for the limoncello but please, whatever you do, ensure you serve this warm and not too hot – you will appreciate the flavour so much more. If your panettone is a little old, don't worry, it will work just as well.

Serves 4

400ml full-fat milk

400ml cream

Zest of 1 unwaxed lemon

50g salted butter, at room temperature

6 slices panettone, about 3cm thick

50g flaked almonds

3 medium eggs

2 egg yolks

45g caster sugar

3 tablespoons limoncello

30g soft brown sugar

Icing sugar for dusting

1 Preheat the oven to 180°C/gas mark 4.

2 Heat the milk and cream with the lemon zest in a medium saucepan and bring to the boil. Remove from the heat and set aside.

3 Meanwhile, butter the panettone and cut each slice into triangles.

4 Sprinkle half the almonds over the base of an ovenproof dish with a 25cm diameter and at least 8cm deep. Neatly overlap the panettone slices over the almonds.

5 Beat together the eggs, egg yolks, sugar and limoncello in a large bowl. Slowly add the milk mixture and mix well. Spoon the mixture over the panettone and leave to soak for about 15 minutes. (The soaking is important because it means the pudding will grow in the oven like a soufflé.)

6 Use your fingers to gently push the panettone slices down into the milk and egg mixture. Sprinkle the top with brown sugar.

7 Place the dish in a roasting tin and pour in enough hot water to come halfway up the sides of the dish.

8 Bake in the middle of the oven for 40 minutes until the custard is lightly set and the top is golden brown. Sprinkle the remaining almonds on top for the last 10 minutes of cooking.

9 Remove the dish from the roasting tin, and leave to rest for 5 minutes. Dust with icing sugar and serve immediately.

TORTA DOLCE DI RISO
Sweet rice cake with limoncello liqueur

Guys, if you like rice pudding you are definitely going to love my sweet rice cake. The lemon zest gives it that refreshing flavour and it's fun to serve squares of cake on cocktail sticks at a tea party. Never attempt to cook this dessert with long-grain rice; it just will not work. Always use a good-quality risotto rice for the perfect result. To get the best flavours, eat it at room temperature. Enjoy!

Serves 8/makes 24

Salted butter for greasing

6 tablespoons fine breadcrumbs

1 litre full-fat milk

200g Arborio or Carnaroli rice

220g caster sugar

6 medium eggs, beaten

130g toasted almonds, roughly chopped

130g candied lemon peel

Zest of 1 unwaxed lemon

5 tablespoons Limoncello liqueur

Icing sugar for dusting

1 Grease an ovenproof rectangular dish, about 30cm long with sides at least 5cm deep. Sprinkle over the breadcrumbs and tap out any excess.

2 Preheat the oven to 180°C/gas mark 4.

3 Pour the milk into a large saucepan and bring to the boil. Add the rice and cook over a low heat for 30 minutes until all the milk is absorbed. Add the caster sugar, mix well and remove from the heat. Leave to cool.

4 Stir in the eggs, almonds, lemon peel and zest and mix everything together. Pour in the limoncello and fold into the mixture.

5 Pour the rice mixture into the prepared dish and bake in the middle of the oven for 1 hour. Remove from the oven and leave to cool.

6 Transfer the rice cake onto a chopping board and with the help of a long sharp knife cut into 5cm squares (you should have 24).

7 Place the rice squares on a large serving dish, dust the tops with icing sugar and serve cold with a little cocktail stick stuck into each square.

LA TORTA DI MAMMA
My mother's upside-down orange sponge

Whenever my parents had a dinner party, my Mamma Alba would always prepare this sponge for the dessert. To be honest with you, as a child I never appreciated the flavours but now, I always beg her to make it for me. The caramelised oranges alone will do. This is definitely one of those desserts that you should place in the centre of the table and let everybody tuck in. Every time I cook it for my friends and family, I hope to enjoy the leftovers with a cup of tea in the morning and I'm always disappointed as there's never any left. If you have a very sweet tooth you can serve it with clotted cream instead of mascarpone cheese.

Serves 8

2 large oranges, peeled and sliced
   in 1cm slices
3 large eggs
120g caster sugar
1 teaspoon baking powder
Zest of 2 unwaxed oranges
125g plain flour
3 tablespoons orange liqueur

FOR THE CARAMEL
210g granulated sugar
3 tablespoons water

1. To prepare the caramel, place the granulated sugar in a small non-stick heavy-based pan with the water. Place over a medium heat and stir until dissolved. Once the sugar mixture is gently boiling and starting to darken, remove the pan from the heat and pour the caramel into a 20cm flan dish.

2. Gently push the orange slices into the caramel slightly overlapping. Do be careful because the caramel will be very hot. Set aside.

3. Preheat the oven to 180°C/gas mark 4.

4. Crack the eggs into a large bowl and whisk until fluffy. Tip in the caster sugar and continue to whisk until creamy and thick.

5. Add in the baking powder and orange zest and continue to whisk until the mixture forms thick ribbons.

6. Gradually sift the flour into the egg mixture and with a large metal spoon, fold in gently to incorporate as much air as possible.

7. Pour the mixture into the flan dish over the caramel sauce and bake in the middle of the oven for 25 minutes. After this time, test it is cooked by inserting a strand of dry spaghetti in the centre of the sponge and if it comes out clean it is ready.

8. Remove the tin from the oven and run a knife round the rim of the sponge to loosen it.

9. Wearing oven gloves, place a flat serving plate over the top of the tin, quickly invert both plate and tin to turn out the orange sponge. (Be careful as the caramel sauce will be very hot.)

10. Drizzle over the orange liqueur and leave to rest at room temperature for 15 minutes.

11. Slice and serve slightly warm with a tablespoon of mascarpone cheese on the side.

PASTIERA DI FORMAGGIO E AMARETTO

Baked cheesecake with amaretto and raisins

If I'm ever invited over to someone's house for a tea party, I'm always secretly hoping that they will have a homemade baked cheesecake. It's filling, tasty and perfect with a cup of tea. Of course you can have many versions but my favourite by far is this one. Ricotta cheese works perfectly with the almond liqueur amaretto and, to me, the best cheesecakes are always the simplest ones.

Serves 8

FOR THE SHORTCRUST PASTRY

1 medium egg yolk

2 tablespoons cold water

180g plain flour plus extra for dusting

Pinch of salt

2 tablespoons caster sugar

1 tablespoon ground almonds

110g salted butter, chilled and diced

FOR THE FILLING

500g ricotta cheese

200ml sour cream

2 medium eggs

2 tablespoons ground almonds

100g icing sugar

5 tablespoons amaretto liqueur

1 tablespoon large raisins

2 tablespoons flaked almonds

1 To make the pastry, place the egg yolk in a small bowl and pour in the water, mix with a fork and set aside.

2 Sift the flour, salt, sugar and ground almonds into a large bowl. Add the butter and rub in with your fingertips until the mixture resembles fine crumbs. Stir in the yolk mixture and work with your fingers to create a firm dough. If the dough looks dry, add a little more cold water.

3 Wrap the dough in clingfilm and leave to rest in the fridge for 30 minutes.

4 Transfer the dough to a lightly floured surface and roll out to a circle about 28cm diameter. Use to line a 22cm loose-based flan tin and prick the base with a fork. Chill for 30 minutes.

5 Preheat the oven to 190°C/gas mark 5.

6 Line the pastry case with greaseproof paper, fill with baking beans and bake in the middle of the oven for 15 minutes. Take the tin out of the oven and let the pastry rest for 5 minutes. Remove the paper and beans and return to the oven for a further 6 minutes until the pastry base is crisp and lightly coloured. Place the flan tin on a baking tray.

7 Reduce the temperature to 150°C/gas mark 2.

8 To prepare the filling, place the ricotta cheese in a large bowl with the sour cream, eggs, almonds, icing sugar and amaretto. Mix all the ingredients together until combined and smooth. Pour the filling into the pastry case and scatter over the raisins and flaked almonds. Bake in the middle of the oven for 70 minutes.

9 Turn off the oven and leave the cheesecake to rest in the oven for 2 hours without opening the door.

10 Unmould the cheesecake, cover with clingfilm and chill in the fridge for at least 8 hours.

11 Remove from the fridge 30 minutes before slicing and serving.

PANE DOLCE DI BANANE

Banana and hazelnut bread

Banana bread is lovely for breakfast or tea but can often be made too stodgy and heavy. My version has a chunky texture as the nuts give it a robust quality while the banana sponge remains light – together they are *fantastico*. If you want it for breakfast, you can prepare this the night before and if wrapped up well in clingfilm, will remain soft for a few days. Make sure your bananas are ripe to get the best flavour out of them.

Serves 6

130g salted butter, at room
 temperature, plus extra
 for greasing

150g soft brown sugar

2 medium eggs, beaten

100g hazelnuts, chopped

3 large very ripe bananas, mashed

240g strong white flour

1 tablespoon baking powder

½ teaspoon grated nutmeg

Pinch of salt

Pinch of freshly ground
 black pepper

1 teaspoon vanilla extract

1 Grease a 1kg loaf tin with butter and line the base with greaseproof paper. Preheat the oven to 180°C/gas mark 4.

3 Cream the butter and sugar in a large bowl until fluffy and pale in colour.

4 Add in the eggs, in 3 stages, whisking well after each addition. Add the hazelnuts and bananas to the mixture.

5 Sift the flour and baking powder onto the mixture and add in the nutmeg, salt and pepper. Pour in the vanilla extract and gently fold everything together until all the ingredients are just incorporated.

6 Transfer the mixture into the loaf tin and bake in the middle of the oven for 55 minutes. After this time, test it is cooked by inserting a strand of dry spaghetti in the centre of the sponge and if it comes out clean and dry it is ready.

7 Turn out the loaf onto a wire rack to cool and enjoy a slice with your afternoon tea.

BABÀ
Rum Babas

In any Italian patisserie, you will always find the classic rum baba. They are normally the size of your fist and shaped like a champagne cork. My father loves baba and last time he visited I made a large cake version and served it to him with fresh fruits. I was in his good books for weeks! You can be creative and use another liqueur like limoncello, but for me the only way is the rum way. As we say in Italian; *U babà e' na cosa seria!*

Makes 12 babas

2 medium eggs

2 tablespoons caster sugar

100g salted butter, melted, plus extra for greasing

150g plain flour

Small pinch of salt

4 teaspoons fast-action dried yeast diluted in 4 teaspoons warm water

FOR THE SYRUP

250ml water

250ml rum

200g caster sugar

1 Grease 12 dariole moulds or deep ramekins with butter.

2 Whisk the eggs and sugar in a large bowl until pale and foamy. Pour in the melted butter and continue to whisk until it is fully incorporated.

3 Add in 100g of the flour with the salt and, with the help of a wooden spoon beat until beautifully creamy. Sprinkle 25g of flour over the top, drizzle in the yeast mixture and cover with the remaining flour. Leave to rest for 15 minutes until the yeast starts to bubble. Continue to beat for 3 minutes, cover with clingfilm and leave to rise in a warm place away from draughts for 25 minutes.

4 Remove the clingfilm from the baba mixture and beat for a further 5 minutes. Pour the mixture into the moulds so it reaches halfway up, and leave to rise again, uncovered, for 25 minutes.

5 Preheat the oven to 150°C/gas mark 2.

6 Cook the babas in the middle of the oven for 15–20 minutes until risen and golden.

7 Remove from the oven and leave to cool. Invert the mould onto a large plate and leave the babas to dry for 24 hours.

8 To make the syrup, put all the ingredients in a large saucepan and bring to the boil. Remove from the heat and leave to one side until warm.

9 Place each baba in the saucepan with the syrup and, with the help of a ladle, drizzle the syrup over the cake. Remove carefully and repeat with the other babas and transfer to serving plates.

10 Serve the babas accompanied with seasonal fresh fruits of your choice.

TORTA DI MELE E MARSALA
Apple and Marsala pie

Having had such great feedback for my *Torta di Mele,* from my previous book *Fantastico!*, I wanted to create something similar for you pie-lovers out there – I'm sure you'll like this one just as much. I have also tried the same recipe using fresh raspberries or rhubarb and it's been a great success. You can substitute the Marsala wine with amaretto liqueur if you prefer. Ensure you serve the tart either warm with cream or ice cream or at room temperature but never straight from the fridge – the cold temperature will ruin its flavours.

Serves 6

1kg cooking apples
50g caster sugar
30g salted butter, melted
Zest of 1 unwaxed orange
3 tablespoons Marsala wine

FOR THE TOPPING
90g self-raising flour
35g plain flour
50g salted butter, cubed
2 tablespoons caster sugar
½ teaspoon ground cinnamon
1 large egg, lightly beaten
3 or so tablespoons full-fat milk
1½ tablespoons demerara sugar

1 Preheat the oven to 180°C/gas mark 4.

2 Peel and core the apples and cut into 8 wedges. Place in a large bowl with the sugar, butter, orange zest and Marsala wine. Mix well until the apples wedges are well coated. Transfer to a 1.5 litre ovenproof dish with sides about 5cm deep.

3 Cover with foil and bake in the middle of the oven for 15 minutes. Remove from the oven, stir, cover with foil again and continue to cook for a further 15 minutes. Meanwhile prepare the topping.

4 Sift the flours into a large bowl, add the butter and rub in with your fingerstips until the mixture resembles fine crumbs. Stir in the sugar and cinnamon and make a well in the centre.

5 Using the handle of a wooden spoon, stir in the egg and enough milk to create a mixture of thick dropping consistency (like a thick yogurt).

6 Remove the dish of cooked apples from the oven and take off the foil.

7 Drop spoonfuls of the topping mixture over the apples, ensuring the surface is completely covered. Sprinkle with the demerara sugar and return the dish to the middle of the oven for 35 minutes. After this time, test it is cooked by inserting a strand of dry spaghetti in the centre of the topping and if it comes out clean and dry it is ready.

8 Serve my apple pie hot with a little double cream on the side.

TORTA DI NONNA ASSUNTA

My grandmother's pear and pine kernel sponge

My grandmother Assunta is well known for her cakes and people in our village are still after her recipes. I was fortunate, as a little boy, to have the chance to cook with her and of course I stole a lot of her ideas and recipes too. It is very important to use ripe pears for this sponge, not the canned ones, and of course, use the freshest eggs you can get.

Serves 8

200g plain flour

1 tablespoon baking powder

200g caster sugar

3 medium eggs

4 teaspoons vanilla extract

Zest of 1 unwaxed lemon

130ml full-fat milk

80g pine kernels

100g salted butter, at room temperature, cut into pieces

2 ripe pears, peeled and cut into eighths, core and pips removed

Icing sugar for dusting (optional)

1 Cover the base and sides of a 25cm baking tin with a sheet of greaseproof paper and preheat the oven to 180°C/gas mark 4.

2 Place the flour, baking powder sugar, eggs, vanilla extract and lemon zest in a large bowl. Pour in the milk and whisk until smooth. Add the pine kernels with the butter and continue to whisk until everything is well combined.

3 Pour the sponge mixture into the prepared tin and arrange the pear slices on top. Gently press the pears into the mixture.

4 Bake in the middle of the oven for 28 minutes until golden.

5 If you wish, dust a little icing sugar on top before serving warm with a cup of coffee or tea.

TORTA DI SORRENTO
The best lemon cake

If you ever get the chance to visit the south of Italy, please try and see the little town of Sorrento. Not only is it extremely picturesque but the food is incredible. Lemons are sold on stalls at the side of the road and some of them are as big as melons. Lemons from Sorrento not only look good, they taste beautiful. This recipe has been passed down to me from my great-grandfather and it is the ultimate lemon cake, even made with 'normal' lemons. If you enjoy tangy fresh flavours this recipe will not disappoint.

Serves 10

150g soft salted butter plus extra for greasing

150g caster sugar

Zest of 2 large unwaxed lemons

3 large eggs

150g self-raising flour

2 tablespoons full-fat milk

1 teaspoon vanilla extract

Icing sugar for dusting

FOR THE SYRUP

100g icing sugar

2 large unwaxed lemons (use the ones you zested)

1 Grease with butter and line a 900g loaf tin and preheat the oven to 160°C/gas mark 3.

2 Cream the butter, caster sugar and lemon zest in a large bowl until soft and light. Whisk the eggs and sift the flour. Gradually add the eggs and flour to the butter mixture. Beat well together.

3 Stir in enough milk, along with the vanilla extract, to make the mixture drop easily from a spoon. Spread the mixture into the prepared tin and bake in the middle of the oven for 45–50 minutes.

4 Remove from the oven and stand the cake, still in its tin, on a wire rack to cool.

5 To make the syrup, gently heat together the icing sugar and lemon juice in a medium saucepan until a syrup forms.

6 Use a fork to prick the top of the warm cake all over. Gently pour the syrup all over the cake and leave to cool completely.

7 Turn out the lemon cake onto a serving plate, dust with icing sugar and enjoy.

LA BELLA CAPRESE
Almond and chocolate cake (wheat-free)

Born and bred on the island of Capri, opposite the bay of Naples, this is the best chocolate cake EVER. It is also a recipe that brings back lots of memories of when I was at catering college and when I was a little boy. In Italy we often make the Bella Caprese to celebrate birthdays or first communions. I clearly remember all my school friends and how many times we baked this cake together. Give it a go and you will soon know what I am talking about.

Serves 8

100g salted butter, plus extra
    for greasing
250g good-quality dark chocolate,
    70% cocoa solids
4 medium eggs, separated
160g icing sugar
150g ground almonds

1 Grease a 23cm loose-based tin and preheat the oven to 180°C/ gas mark 4.

2 Place the butter and chocolate in a large glass bowl over a pan of simmering water and allow to melt. Ensure that the water in the pan doesn't touch the bowl otherwise the chocolate will become bitter.

3 Whisk the egg yolks and icing sugar in a second large bowl until fluffy and pale in colour.

4 In a separate large, spotlessly clean dry bowl, whisk the egg whites until stiff.

5 Pour the melted chocolate into the bowl with the egg yolks and sugar and combine thoroughly. Mix in the ground almonds then immediately fold in the egg whites gently using a metal spoon.

6 Pour the cake mixture into the tin and cook in the middle of the oven for 25–30 minutes.

7 Remove the Caprese from the oven and leave it rest for 10 minutes before unmoulding.

8 Slice and serve at room temperature with a tablespoon of clotted cream and a little glass of amaretto liqueur.

PASTIERA NAPOLETANA

Neapolitan Easter tart with ricotta cheese and candied fruits

Easter in Naples is celebrated with three things; Easter eggs, roasted belly of pork and *pastiera Napoletana*. I remember as a little boy I was more excited about this tart than Easter eggs and today I bake it at least three or four times a year. *Grano cotto* – cooked grains – is a delicacy that works deliciously with the ricotta cheese and orange flower water. I have a confession though: it's my mother who makes the best one ever!

Serves 10

FOR THE PASTRY

350g plain flour

200g unsalted butter, at room temperature, plus extra for greasing

2 teaspoons vanilla extract

2 large eggs

100g caster sugar

A little milk if needed

FOR THE FILLING

500g ricotta cheese

150g caster sugar

4 large egg yolks

2 teaspoons orange flower water

120g candied fruits, finely chopped

850g jar or canned *grano cotto* (cooked grains, available from Italian delis and online)

1   Grease a 28cm tart tin, with sides at least 5cm deep, with butter, and line it with greaseproof paper.

2   To prepare the pastry, place the flour, butter and vanilla extract in a large bowl. Rub together using your fingertips until the mixture resembles fine breadcrumbs.

3   Add the eggs and sugar and use your hands to mix and form a firm dough. If the dough is a little dry, add a tablespoon of milk and blend together. Cover the dough with clingfilm and leave it to rest in the fridge for 20 minutes.

4   Preheat the oven to 180°C/gas mark 4.

5   To make the filling, put the ricotta cheese in a large bowl with the sugar and mix with a fork. Add in the egg yolks, orange flower water, candied fruits and *grano cotto* and mix all the ingredients together.

6   Roll out the pastry on a well-floured surface until about 5mm thick. Use it to line the prepared tart tin and spoon in the ricotta mixture.

7   Gather up and re-roll the pastry trimmings and cut them into 2cm-wide strips. Lay the strips in rows about 3cm apart over the top of the tart. Give the tart a quarter turn and repeat the process to create a lattice.

8   Bake in the middle of the oven for 50 minutes.

9   Once cooked, leave the tart to rest out of the oven for 10 minutes before unmoulding.

10   Serve at room temperature.

TORTA LEGGERA AL CIOCCOLATO E ANANAS

Low-fat chocolate and pineapple cake

If you are looking for a dessert that you are not going to feel really guilty about eating, this is the one for you: low-fat chocolate and pineapple cake! You can use canned peaches instead of the pineapple if you prefer and for extra flavour, add in a little more cinnamon.

Serves 8

150g low fat-spread plus extra for greasing

130g caster sugar

½ teaspoon ground cinnamon

1½ teaspoons baking powder

2 medium eggs

100g self-raising flour

3 tablespoons cocoa powder

230g canned pineapple pieces in natural juice

130g low-fat thick natural yogurt

1 tablespoon icing sugar

1 chocolate flake, crushed, for decoration

1 Lightly grease a 20cm square cake tin and line the base and sides with greaseproof paper.

2 Preheat the oven to 190°C/gas mark 5.

3 Put the spread, sugar, cinnamon, baking powder and eggs in a large bowl. Sift over the flour and cocoa powder. Beat with an electric whisk until the mixture is smooth.

4 Pour the cake mixture into the prepared tin and level the surface.

5 Bake in the middle of the oven for 25 minutes. Leave to cool slightly in the tin before transferring to a wire rack to cool completely.

6 Drain the pineapple pieces well, reserve a quarter of them on a plate and place the rest in a medium bowl. Pour over the yogurt, sift in the icing sugar and gently fold everything together.

7 Spoon the pineapple mixture over the chocolate sponge and decorate the top with the reserved pineapple pieces.

8 Sprinkle over the crushed chocolate and enjoy.

ZUCCOTTO CALDO AL CIOCCOLATO

Hot chocolate pudding with amaretto and chocolate sauce

This recipe is definitely for the chocoholics out there or those who really want to impress friends and family. It is the ultimate chocolate pudding. It is so rich and tasty and yet still light and in our house it has been known to be eaten for breakfast when no one was looking. If you are a chocolate person – you will be in heaven with this one. Don't worry about the calories, just work them off!

Serves 6

130g dark chocolate, 70% cocoa solids, broken into pieces

100g salted butter plus extra for greasing

100g soft brown sugar

3 medium eggs, separated

2 teaspoons vanilla extract

130g self-raising flour

1 tablespoon cocoa powder

½ teaspoon bicarbonate of soda

60ml full-fat milk

2 tablespoons amaretto liqueur

Icing sugar for decoration

FOR THE SAUCE

130g dark chocolate, 70% cocoa solids, broken into pieces

60ml double cream

1 tablespoon amaretto liqueur

1 Grease a 1.2 litre pudding basin with butter and line the base with a circle of greaseproof paper. Preheat the oven to 180°C/gas mark 4.

2 Place the chocolate in a medium glass bowl over a pan of simmering water and allow to melt. Ensure that the water in the pan doesn't touch the bowl otherwise the chocolate will become bitter. Leave to cool.

3 Cream the butter in a large bowl with half the sugar until light and creamy. Whisk in the egg yolks with the cooled melted chocolate and vanilla extract. Sift over the flour with the cocoa powder and bicarbonate of soda. Fold into the mixture with a large metal spoon. Finally pour in the milk and amaretto liqueur and fold through.

4 Whisk the egg whites in a large, spotlessly clean dry bowl until soft peaks form. Gradually whisk in the remaining sugar until stiff and glossy. Gently fold the whites into the chocolate mixture.

5 Pour the mixture into the lined basin and cover tightly with foil. Secure with a string and place in a deep oven tray. Pour enough hot water into the tray to come halfway up the sides of the basin.

6 Bake in the middle of the oven for 1 hour and 15 minutes. (After this time, test it is cooked by inserting a strand of dry spaghetti in the centre of the pudding – and if it comes out clean it is ready).

7 Prepare the chocolate sauce by combining all the ingredients in a medium glass bowl over a pan of simmering water. Allow to melt, stirring until smooth.

8 Take the pudding out of the oven and remove the foil.

9 Wearing oven gloves, place a flat serving plate over the top of the pudding basin, quickly invert plate and basin and turn out the chocolate pudding. (Be careful as the pudding will be very hot).

10 Dust the top of the pudding with icing sugar, slice and serve hot with the chocolate sauce poured over.

PANE AL CIOCCOLATO E CANNELLA
Chocolate and cinnamon cake

My youngest son Rocco is a chocoholic and can eat chocolate with almost everything. We came up with this cake together when trying out some of my recipes and he just loves it. You can substitute the chocolate chips with white chocolate if you prefer or try a mixture of both. Delicious warm or cold with a glass of milk, just in case you have a Rocco in the family too!

Serves 6

15g fresh yeast

250ml water, warm

340g strong white flour plus extra for dusting

30g cocoa powder, unsweetened

1 teaspoon ground cinnamon

2 pinches of salt

30g caster sugar

25g salted butter, softened

80g good-quality chocolate, coarsely chopped

Melted butter for brushing

1   Brush a 15cm cake tin with butter and oil the inside of a large bowl.

2   Melt the yeast into the water, making sure that it is completely dissolved.

3   Sift the flour, cocoa powder, cinnamon and salt into a large bowl, sprinkle over the sugar and make a well in the centre. Pour in the water and yeast and gently mix all the ingredients together to form a dough.

4   Work in the soft butter then turn out the dough onto a lightly floured surface. Knead for 5 minutes until smooth and elastic and shape into a ball.

5   Place the dough ball into the oiled bowl and cover with clingfilm. Leave it to rise in a warm place away from draughts for 1 hour.

6   Turn out the dough onto a lightly floured surface and punch down. Gently knead in the chocolate pieces. Shape again into a ball and place in the prepared tin. Cover with clingfilm and leave it to rise in a warm place away from draughts for 50 minutes, by which time the dough should reach the top of the tin.

7   Preheat the oven to 220°C/gas mark 7.

8   Bake in the middle of the oven for 10 minutes. Lower the temperature to 190°C/gas mark 5 and continue to bake for a further 30 minutes.

9   Once out of the oven, brush the top with melted butter and leave the bread in the tin for 10 minutes then turn out onto a wire rack to cool.

10 Perfect served at room temperature for breakfast or afternoon tea.

TORTA FACILE AL CIOCCOLATO (SENZA FARINA)

Simple chocolate cake (wheat-free)

My niece Ella has a wheat allergy and it made me realise that today many people are similarly allergic. I wanted to come up with a chocolate cake that everyone could enjoy and this one is not only wheat-free but really easy to make and absolutely delicious. It's a simple chocolate cake that screams tea parties and can definitely be served warm with any ice cream of your choice. Please use good-quality fresh eggs as it will make a big difference in flavour.

Serves 10

380g good-quality chocolate, 70% cocoa solids

170g unsalted butter plus extra for greasing

6 large eggs, separated

150g caster sugar

3 teaspoons vanilla extract

Pinch of salt

1 Grease a 22cm springform cake tin with butter and line the base and sides with greaseproof paper. Preheat the oven to 180°C/gas mark 4.

2 Place the chocolate and butter in a small saucepan and place over a low heat. Stir until melted and leave to cool, stirring frequently.

3 Put the egg yolks in a large bowl and pour over half the sugar. Whisk together until pale and thick.

4 Slowly fold the warm chocolate mixture into the egg yolks, and then fold in the vanilla extract.

5 Put the egg whites in a large, spotlessly clean dry bowl with the salt and whisk until soft peaks form. Gradually add in the remaining sugar and continue to whisk until firm peaks form.

6 Use a large metal spoon to gently fold the egg whites into the chocolate mixture a little at a time.

7 Pour the mixture into the prepared cake tin and bake in the middle of the oven for 50 minutes.

8 The cake will be cooked once the top is puffed and slightly cracked. If you insert a dry spaghetti strand into the centre it should come out with moist crumbs attached.

9 Enjoy warm with a cup of your favourite tea.

MATTONCINI AL CIOCCOLATO
Sticky chocolate and pecan brownies

For me the ultimate sweet combination is chocolate and nuts so I had to have a cake in this book that combined the two. The gooey softness of this brownie with the crunchiness of pecan nuts is amazing. I love my mattoncini warm or at room temperature with a cup of tea or coffee. Instead of pecan nuts you can use pistachio nuts or hazelnuts if you prefer. Ensure you use a strong white flour for the mixture – this will help to give the brownies that gorgeous chewy texture.

Serves 8

100g salted butter plus extra
    for greasing
170g caster sugar
80g dark muscovado sugar
130g dark chocolate,
    70% cocoa solids
1 tablespoon golden syrup
2 medium eggs
2 tablespoons orange liqueur
110g strong white flour
2 tablespoons cocoa powder
½ teaspoon baking powder
50g pecan nuts, chopped

1 Grease a 20cm shallow square cake tin with butter and line the base with greaseproof paper. Preheat the oven to 180°C/gas mark 4.

2 Place the butter, sugars, chocolate and golden syrup in a medium heavy-based saucepan. Place over a low heat and stir until the mixture is well blended and smooth. Remove from the heat and leave to cool.

3 Beat the eggs with the orange liqueur in a large bowl until fluffy.

4 Pour in the cooled chocolate mixture and whisk until it is well combined.

5 Sift the flour, cocoa powder and baking powder over the mixture. Add the pecan nuts and fold everything together using a metal spoon.

6 Spoon the mixture into the prepared tin and bake in the middle of the oven for 25 minutes. Once cooked the top will be crisp and the edges of the cake will shrink away from the tin.

7 Leave the cake to cool completely in the tin before cutting into squares to serve.

TORTA DI RICOTTA E CAFFÈ
Coffee and ricotta tart

Every Italian loves coffee but I have decided to dedicate this recipe to my good friend Peter Andre. I have never met another man that loves coffee more than I do, so this delicious coffee and ricotta tart is especially for those of you who are like us. The creamy ricotta cheese paired with the strong coffee is amazing.

Serves 10

FOR THE SWEET PASTRY
190g plain flour

100g unsalted butter, cubed, plus extra for greasing

2 tablespoons caster sugar

3 tablespoons water, cold

FOR THE FILLING
1 tablespoon instant coffee

1 tablespoon water

2 tablespoons Baileys liqueur

1.25kg ricotta cheese

120g caster sugar

2 tablespoons plain flour

Pinch of salt

120g dark chocolate, 70% cocoa solids, finely chopped, plus an extra 50g for decoration

4 medium egg yolks

½ teaspoon vegetable or sunflower oil

1 Grease a 25cm springform tin with butter.

2 To prepare the pastry, sift the flour in a large bowl. Add the butter and rub in with your fingertips until the mixture resembles fine crumbs. Stir in the sugar then pour in the cold water. Pinch with your fingers to form a dough and, if it seems dry, add a little more water. Transfer the dough to a lightly floured surface and gather together into a ball. Cover with clingfilm and leave it to rest in the fridge for 10 minutes.

3 Place the rested dough on a lightly floured surface and roll out to a thickness of ½cm. Line the tin so that the pastry comes about two-thirds of the way up the sides. Cover with clingfilm and refrigerate while preparing the filling.

4 Put the instant coffee in a cup and dissolve in the water and Baileys. Set aside.

5 Place the ricotta cheese in a large bowl and add the sugar, flour and salt. Mix everything together until smooth. Pour in the coffee mixture, the chopped chocolate and egg yolks. Stir until well mixed.

6 Spoon the filling into the pastry shell and smooth the top. Cover with clingfilm and chill for 45 minutes.

7 Preheat the oven to 180°C/gas mark 4.

8 Place the tin on a baking tray and bake in the middle of the oven for 1 hour. Turn off the oven, slightly open the door and leave the tart to cool in the oven.

9 Place the remaining 50g of chocolate in a small saucepan and pour over the oil. Stir and melt over a very low heat.

10 Remove the tart from the oven and unmould onto a serving plate. With the help of a fork, drizzle over the melted chocolate.

11 Slice and serve at room temperature with a nice cup of coffee.

ZUCCOTTO AL MARSALA

Chocolate and hazelnut ice cream in a Marsala sponge shell

For those of you who have never made an ice-cream cake, you will probably think that it would be impossible to tackle at home. That is just not the case – you will be surprised at just how easy it is! This is a traditional northern Italian cake that will satisfy you in every way. You can substitute the Marsala wine with port or a dessert wine if you prefer, and do buy good-quality chocolate as it will make all the difference to the taste.

Serves 8

FOR THE SPONGE

4 medium eggs

150g caster sugar

1 teaspoon vanilla extract

150g plain flour plus extra
    for dusting

Butter for greasing

FOR THE FILLING

450ml double cream

60g icing sugar

130g good-quality chocolate 70%
    cocoa solids, roughly chopped

130g hazelnuts, roughly chopped

150ml Marsala wine

100ml water, cold

1 Grease a 22cm springform tin with butter and dust it with flour, tapping out any excess. Preheat the oven to 180°C/gas mark 4.

2 To prepare the sponge, whisk the eggs and sugar in a large bowl for 15 minutes with an electric whisk until pale and very fluffy. Pour in the vanilla extract.

3 Sift the flour onto the egg mixture and quickly fold in with a large metal spoon. Once all the flour has been incorporated, pour the mixture into the tin and bake in the middle of the oven for 40 minutes. Remove from the oven and place on a wire rack to cool in the tin.

4 To make the filling, pour the cream in a large bowl, sift in the icing sugar and whip until fluffy. Gently fold in the chocolate, hazelnuts and 1 tablespoon of Marsala wine. Let it rest into the fridge for 15 minutes.

5 Pour the remaining Marsala wine into a bowl and pour over the cold water. Mix together and set aside.

6 Line a 1.5 litre round bowl with a large sheet of clingfilm. Cut the sponge into 1cm slices and use them to line the bowl (reserve those you don't need for the lid). Brush the Marsala and water mixture evenly over the sponge.

7 Pour the cream mixture into the centre of the bowl and gently knock the bowl on the worktop to release any air bubbles.

8 Enclose the cream mixture with a lid of sponge slices soaked in the remaining Marsala and water.

9 Cover the *zuccotto* with clingfilm and freeze for 4 hours.

10 Before serving, place the *zuccotto* in the fridge for at least 1 hour.

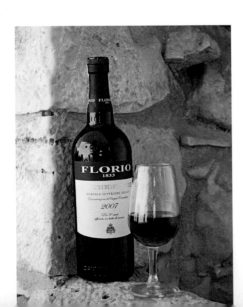

BISCUITS

AMARETTI MORBIDI
Soft amaretti biscuits

If the D'Acampo family have tea, it will always be accompanied with freshly made amaretti biscuits. Of course these little treats go just as perfectly with a cup of coffee and let me tell you that they are the easiest biscuits you will ever make. If you want to keep my amaretti soft, store them in a sealed container for three or four days; otherwise, enjoy them firm – try a couple crumbled on top of your favourite ice cream.

Serves 4

Salted butter for greasing
4 medium egg whites
350g caster sugar
350g ground almonds
30ml amaretto liqueur
Icing sugar for dusting

1 Line a baking tray with greaseproof paper and lightly grease with butter. Preheat the oven to 180°C/gas mark 4.

2 Whisk the egg whites in a large, spotlessly clean dry bowl until stiff and firm. Gently mix in the sugar and almonds. Pour in the amaretto liqueur and fold in carefully to make a smooth paste.

3 Use a teaspoon to place small heaps of the mixture on the lined tray, spacing them about 3cm apart to allow for expansion during cooking.

4 Bake in the middle of the oven for about 15 minutes until golden brown.

5 Enjoy the biscuits warm or leave them to dry on a wire rack until crisp and firm.

6 Dust with a little icing sugar and serve with coffee or ice cream.

BISCOTTI AL BURRO
Butter and semolina biscuits

A lot of people are scared of using semolina but used in the right way it is a great ingredient. My biscuits are lovely in texture and the butter gives them a rich creamy flavour. I served them warm with ice cream and it was a success. Do use salted butter as it adds a pleasant little saltiness to the biscuits. *Buonissimo!*

Serves 4

100g plain flour
50g fine semolina
100g salted butter plus extra
    for greasing
50g caster sugar plus extra
    for dusting

1 Lightly grease a baking tray with butter and preheat the oven to 160°C/gas mark 3.

2 Place the flour and semolina in a large bowl. Add the butter and sugar and rub everything together with your fingertips. As soon as the mixture begins to bind together, lightly knead to create a smooth dough.

3 Transfer the dough to the greased baking tray and roll out to an 18cm circle.

4 Prick the surface all over with a fork and crimp the edges for an attractive finish. Use a table knife to mark the circle into 8 wedges. Put the dough to rest in the fridge for about 20 minutes until firm.

5 Bake in the middle of the oven for 40 minutes until beautifully golden.

6 Remove from the oven and immediately re-mark the wedges with the knife while the biscuit is still hot, then dust with caster sugar. Leave to cool on the baking tray for 5 minutes.

7 With the help of a pallet knife, carefully lift the biscuit circle off the tray and place on a wire rack to cool completely.

8 Cut into wedges and serve 2 wedges per portion with your favourite vanilla ice cream.

BISCOTTI DI POLENTA E UVA SULTANINA

Polenta cookies with sultanas

I have had so many different reactions to polenta, some of you love it, and some of you hate it. I wanted to come up with something that everyone would love and I think this is the one. The sweetness of the biscuit with the raisins is amazing, served warm or cold. Perfect with an espresso and fantastic to pack into a lunchbox.

Makes about 50 cookies

100g sultanas
3 medium egg yolks
100g caster sugar
140g plain flour
160g fine polenta
½ teaspoon baking powder
150g salted butter, melted
Icing sugar for dusting

1   Line a large baking tray with greaseproof paper.

2   Place the sultanas in a small bowl and cover in hot water for 20 minutes. Drain and set aside.

3   Whisk the egg yolks and sugar in a large bowl until pale and fluffy.

4   Sift the flours and baking powder over the egg mixture. Use a wooden spoon to beat in the melted butter. Fold in the drained sultanas and mix all the ingredients together.

5   Divide the mixture onto 2 large pieces of greaseproof paper and shape into 2 cylinders about 5cm in diameter. Leave the rolls to rest into the fridge for 2 hours.

6   Preheat the oven to 180°C/gas mark 4.

7   Cut the chilled rolls into 1cm thick discs and lay them on the lined baking tray. Do not place the cookies too close to each other as they will expand during cooking.

8   Bake in the middle of the oven for 15 minutes until beautifully golden.

9   Leave the cookies in the tray and cool on a wire rack.

10 Dust the tops with icing sugar and serve.

BISCOTTI ALL'UOVO CON MARMELLATA
Egg cookies with apricot jam

Biscuits are a massive item on our shopping list, especially when my brother-in-law Orlando comes to visit from Naples – we have to ensure that we have at least six different packets in the house (and they probably will last only a couple of days). When I go home to Italy, though, I get my sister to make these jam biscuits as there is nothing better than the smell, texture and taste of a freshly made biscuit. You can use any jam of your choice and it works wonderfully with chocolate spread too.

Makes about 30 cookies

3 medium eggs
150g plain flour
90g caster sugar
50g salted butter, softened
1 teaspoon vanilla extract
2 tablespoons full-fat milk
5 tablespoons apricot jam

1   Line a large baking tray with greaseproof paper.

2   Place the eggs in a small saucepan and boil for 10 minutes until hard. Cool under cold running water and peel. Discard the whites and sieve the yolks into a large bowl.

3   Sift the flour and sugar into the bowl with the egg yolks. Add the butter and vanilla extract. Pour in the milk and mix all the ingredients together for 5 minutes until you have a dough.

4   Place the dough onto a large sheet of greaseproof paper and roll it into a log about 3cm in diameter. Leave the log to rest in the fridge for 45 minutes.

5   Preheat the oven to 180°C/gas mark 4.

6   Cut the cold log into pieces about the size of a walnut. Gently use your hands to roll them into small balls.

7   Place the balls on the baking paper and use your thumb to make an indentation in the centre of each ball.

8   Fill each hole with a little apricot jam using a teaspoon.

9   Bake in the middle of the oven for 15 minutes until beautifully golden.

10 Remove from the oven and leave to cool on a wire rack. Serve at room temperature.

BISCOTTINI SPEZIATI
Crispy spiced Sicilian biscuits

Cheese and biscuits after a dinner party are a must in the D'Acampos' house and if you are looking for a biscuit full of flavour that can complement your cheese, please bake these. The spicy warm ginger flavours are amazing and work beautifully with blue cheeses. These Sicilian biscuits are simply the best and your guests will be highly impressed.

Makes about 25 biscuits

110g plain flour
¼ teaspoon ground ginger
½ teaspoon mixed spice
¼ teaspoon ground cinnamon
½ teaspoon bicarbonate of soda
60g salted butter, soft plus extra
    for greasing
50g caster sugar
2 tablespoons golden syrup, warm

1 Lightly grease 2 baking trays and preheat the oven to 180°C/gas mark 4.

2 Sift the flour, spices and bicarbonate of soda into a large bowl. Add the butter and rub in with your fingerstips until the mixture resembles fine crumbs. Mix in the sugar and pour over the golden syrup. Combine all the ingredients to create a soft dough.

3 Roll the mixture into balls, about the same size of marble balls.

4 Place all the balls on the prepared trays, allowing at least 5cm between them as they will expand during cooking.

5 Bake in the middle of the oven for 10 minutes. Remove the trays from the oven and band them down on a solid workface – this causes the biscuits to crack and spread. Continue to bake for a further 5 minutes until golden brown in colour.

6 Cool on a wire rack and enjoy the Sicilian biscuits with a selection of strong cheeses of your choice.

CANTUCCINI CLASSICI

Double-baked biscuits with almond and pistachio nuts

I always have a selection of nuts in my storecupboard because they are so good for us, releasing many healthy fats that our bodies thrive on. Cantuccini are one of the most popular biscuits in Italy and traditionally are double baked to give an extra crunch. You will often find a cantuccini biscuit served with your coffee in an Italian restaurant but to me, it's perfect with any ice cream.

Makes about 20 cantuccini

90g whole almonds, skinned
90g shelled pistachio nuts
250g strong white flour
150g caster sugar
1 teaspoon baking powder
2 large eggs, beaten
1 teaspoon vanilla extract
Zest of 1 unwaxed orange
Icing sugar for dusting

1   Line 1 or 2 baking trays with greaseproof paper and preheat the oven to 180°C/gas mark 4.

2   Tip the almonds into a small frying pan over a medium heat and toast them. Toss the almonds occasionally to ensure they turn an even golden brown. Set aside.

3   Put the pistachios in a medium bowl and pour over boiling water from the kettle. Leave the pistachios to soak for 2 minutes then drain and peel off the skin. Set aside.

4   Sift the flour, sugar and baking powder into a large bowl. Stir in the nuts with the eggs, vanilla extract and orange zest and combine to form a biscuit dough.

5   Dust your work surface with icing sugar, divide the dough into 3 pieces and shape each piece into a sausage by rolling it with your hands in the icing sugar.

6   Place the rolls on the prepared baking tray and flatten slightly.

7   Bake for 20 minutes in the middle of the oven.

8   Remove from the oven and place the rolls on a chopping board. Use a sharp knife to cut each roll diagonally into 1cm strips.

9   Spread the strips in a single layer on the baking tray and return to the oven for 3 minutes. (You may need an extra tray for the second baking).

10 Leave the cantuccini to cool on a wire rack before serving. Enjoy them with your favourite ice cream or a little glass of Vin Santo.

MERENGHINE CON PISTACCHIO
Little pistachio meringues

I often make a hazelnut and raspberry meringue cake and love the taste of a nutty meringue, that's how I came up with this biscuit. I was experimenting with some leftover pistachio nuts one day and ended up creating this recipe. These mini meringues will not disappoint your guests. They look impressive and have to be one of the easiest biscuits to prepare from this book. You can also create an Eton Mess with them IF you have any left over. If you prefer, use hazelnuts instead of the pistachio nuts.

Makes about 30 meringues

4 large egg whites

115g caster sugar

115g icing sugar

50g shelled pistachio nuts, very finely chopped

1   Line 2 baking trays with greaseproof paper and preheat the oven to 110°C/gas mark ¼.

2   Pour the egg whites into a large, spotlessly clean dry glass or metal bowl. On a medium speed, beat with an electric whisk until stiff and firm.

3   Increase the beater speed and start to add in the caster sugar, a spoonful at a time. Continue beating for 5 seconds between each addition. When you finished adding the caster sugar, the mixture should be thick and glossy.

4   Sift a third of the icing sugar over the mixture and gently fold in with a large metal spoon. Continue the process until all the icing sugar is incorporated. Do not overmix.

5   Lastly, gently fold in the pistachio nuts.

6   Scoop out a tablespoon of the mixture at a time and place on the lined trays, creating rough rounds.

7   Bake in the middle of the oven for 80 minutes. You will know the meringues are ready if they sound crisp when tapped underneath.

8   Leave the meringues to cool on a wire rack and enjoy them with some whipped cream and seasonal fresh fruit.

ANELLI AL LIMONCELLO

Pistachio and limoncello rings

Limoncello in Sorrento is like gravy and chips in Manchester. You will always be offered a limoncello liqueur after your meal because it's fantastic for the digestion. I absolutely love its intense lemon flavour in food and have often used it in trifles and sponges. I wanted to see if it would work in a biscuit format and it really does. If you like lemon, try these traditional southern Italian biscuits that have that unexpected kick.

Makes 20 rings

180g salted butter, at room temperature, plus extra for greasing

50g caster sugar

230g plain flour, sifted

1 tablespoon full-fat milk

130g icing sugar, sifted

2 tablespoons limoncello liqueur

50g shelled pistachio nuts, chopped

1 Grease a large baking tray with butter and preheat the oven to 180°C/ gas mark 4.

2 Cream the butter and sugar in a large bowl until light and pale. With the help of a wooden spoon, stir in the flour and milk until you have a fairly soft dough. If it seems dry, add a little more milk.

3 Place the mixture into a piping bag fitted with a 1cm star nozzle.

4 Pipe the mixture into 5cm rings on the greased baking tray, spacing them well apart.

5 Bake in the middle of the oven for 10 minutes until beautifully golden. Transfer the biscuits to a wire rack to cool slightly.

6 Put the icing sugar in a small bowl and pour in enough limoncello to create a thin icing. Brush the icing over the biscuits while still warm.

7 Finally, sprinkle the chopped pistachio all over the biscuits and leave to set before serving.

8 Perfect served with a cup of tea.

BISCOTTI ALLA VANIGLIA E CIOCCOLATO

Chocolate chip and vanilla cookies

Like all children, my boys love cooking. I caught my wife and kids once making cookies from a ready-made packet which just required the adding of an egg or water – you can only imagine my reaction! The whole cooking experience is also weighing and measuring ingredients and learning as you go – there really is no excuse not to try and cook from scratch and this recipe is so easy, I challenge ANYONE to do it. You can vary the recipe by adding in milk or white chocolate chips or a mixture of both.

Serves 8–10

125g dark chocolate chips
125g soft margarine plus extra
   for greasing
60g caster sugar
90g muscovado sugar
1 medium egg
½ teaspoon vanilla extract
175g plain flour
1 teaspoon baking powder

1. Grease a large baking tray with the margarine and preheat the oven to 190°C/gas mark 5.

2. Put all the ingredients in a large glass bowl and mix furiously until well combined.

3. Spoon out heaped tablespoons of the mixture onto the baking tray, spaced well apart. (This amount creates big biscuits, if you prefer smaller ones then prepare 2 large baking trays and use heaped teaspoons of the mixture).

4. Bake in the middle of the oven for 10 minutes.

5. Remove and allow to cool slightly.

6. Enjoy warm.

BISCOTTI SEMPLICI AL CIOCCOLATO
Simple chocolate macaroons

I absolutely love macaroons, the crunchiness on the outside and the chewiness on the inside is delicious. Chocolate in my house is a must and I'll be lying if I say that only my children eat it. These homemade biscuits are really impressive and will not disappoint: adults enjoy the chewy nutty flavour and kids love the chocolate (or is it the other way round!?). Ensure that the chocolate has at least 70 per cent cocoa solids.

Serves 8–10

2 egg whites

225g caster sugar

175g ground almonds

225g good-quality dark chocolate, at least 70% cocoa solids

Butter for greasing

1 Grease a large baking tray with butter and preheat the oven to 180°C/gas mark 4.

2 In a large, spotlessly clean dry bowl, whisk the egg whites until stiff then gently fold in the ground almonds and sugar.

3 Wet your hands, take a tablespoon of the mixture and roll into a finger shape about 6cm long.

4 Place on the baking tray and repeat the process, spacing them well apart.

5 Bake in the middle of the oven for 15–20 minutes until beautifully golden. Remove from the oven and allow to cool slightly.

6 Meanwhile, place the chocolate in a small glass bowl over a pan of simmering water and allow to melt (ensure the bowl does not touch the water otherwise the chocolate will become bitter).

7 Dip the base of each finger biscuit in the chocolate and place on a baking sheet (chocolate side face-up) until set.

8 Once set, turn the biscuits over and with the help of a fork, drizzle over more chocolate sauce creating a zig-zag effect. Alternatively, you may prefer instead just to dip half of the biscuit on one side.

10 Serve once the chocolate has set, with a cup of coffee.

PASTA

MACCHERONI AI QUATTRO FORMAGGI
Maccheroni with four cheeses

My son Rocco doesn't really like milk but loves cheese so when making a traditional maccheroni cheese, I add in as much calcium as possible with many different cheeses. The result? A fantastic rich sauce loved by the whole family. Sometimes I include fried pancetta and, if you are vegetarian, you could add in sliced button mushrooms. Do not use buffalo mozzarella as it releases too much milk and will make the pasta soggy.

Serves 4

300g dried penne rigate

150ml double cream

100g strong Cheddar cheese, grated

100g Gorgonzola, cut into small chunks

½ teaspoon paprika

2 mozzarella balls, drained and cut into chunks

3 egg yolks

150g frozen peas, defrosted

100g freshly grated Parmesan cheese

Salt to taste

1   Preheat the oven to 200°C/gas mark 6.

2   Fill a large saucepan at least three-quarters full with water. Add in 2 tablespoons of salt and bring to the boil. Cook the pasta in the boiling water until al dente, stirring every minute or so. To get the al dente perfect bite, cook the pasta for 1 minute less than indicated in the packet instructions. Drain and return the pasta to the same pan, away from the heat.

3   Pour in the cream, along with the Cheddar and Gorgonzola cheeses. Put the saucepan back over a very low heat and with the help of a wooden spoon start to mix the ingredients together for 30 seconds.

4   Take the pan off the heat again and add the paprika, mozzarella, egg yolks, peas and half the Parmesan cheese. Season with a little salt and stir everything together for 30 seconds.

5   Tip the pasta into a 25cm round ovenproof dish (or similar sized rectangular one) with sides at least 5cm deep. Sprinkle the top with the remaining Parmesan.

6   Bake in the middle of the oven for 20 minutes until it is bubbling and blistering on top.

7   Leave the maccheroni to rest out of the oven for 3 minutes before serving to your friends and family.

CANNELLONI TRADIZIONALI
Cannelloni filled with spinach and ricotta cheese

This is vegetarian pasta bake at its best, with not many ingredients to buy. I have tried this recipe with shop-bought béchamel sauce and it still tasted beautiful, although of course try to make a fresh one if you can.

Serves 6–8

720ml passata (sieved tomatoes)

15 basil leaves

26 fresh egg pasta sheets cut into 7 x 15cm rectangles

30g freshly grated Parmesan cheese

Salt and pepper to taste

FOR THE BÉCHAMEL SAUCE

100g salted butter

100g plain flour

1 litre full-fat milk, cold

¼ freshly grated nutmeg

FOR THE FILLING

500g ricotta cheese

300g frozen spinach, defrosted and squeezed of excess water

¼ teaspoon freshly grated nutmeg

60g freshly grated Parmesan cheese

Salt and pepper to taste

1 Preheat the oven to 180°C/gas mark 4.

2 Pour the passata into a large bowl with the basil leaves. Season with salt and pepper, mix all the ingredients together and set aside.

3 To make the béchamel sauce, melt the butter in a large saucepan over a medium heat. Stir in the flour and cook for 1 minute until it turns a light brown colour. Gradually whisk in the cold milk, lower the heat and cook for 10 minutes whisking constantly. Once thickened, stir in the nutmeg. Season with salt and pepper and set aside to cool slightly.

4 To prepare the filling, place all the ingredients in a large bowl, season with salt and pepper and use a fork to mix everything together.

5 Place 1½ tablespoons of filling onto each pasta sheet and start to roll up the pasta from the narrow side going forward. To seal the cannellone, overlap the pasta sheet by about 2cm. Repeat the process until all the pasta sheets are filled.

6 Select a rectangular ovenproof dish measuring 25 x 35cm and pour in a third of the béchamel sauce. Spread evenly over the base.

7 Place half the filled cannelloni on the béchamel layer with the seam facing down.

8 Spoon over half the passata and half of the remaining béchamel sauce.

9 Build up a second layer of cannelloni and spoon over the remaining passata. Spread over the remaining béchamel sauce.

10 Finish by sprinkling over the Parmesan cheese and bake in the middle of the oven for 30 minutes or until coloured and crispy.

11 Remove the dish from the oven and leave to rest for 5 minutes. This makes it easier to cut and serve as the layers hold together better.

LASAGNE CON VERDURE
Vegetable lasagne

In my house, we eat lasagne at least once a week and my boys prefer it made with aubergines rather than peppers, but to be honest, in a lasagne anything goes. You can place in the middle some sliced mozzarella, if you fancy it cheesier or even use Cheddar cheese in the béchamel – as I said, anything goes.

Serves 8

4 tablespoons olive oil

2 large red onions, peeled and finely sliced

2 celery sticks, cut into 1cm cubes

200g courgettes, cut into 1cm cubes

100g carrots, peeled and cut into 1cm cubes

3 red peppers, cut into 1cm cubes

3 yellow peppers, cut into 1cm cubes

1 glass of Italian dry white wine

2 x 400g cans chopped tomatoes

1 tablespoon tomato purée

10 basil leaves

9 fresh lasagne sheets (each about 10 x 18cm)

60g freshly grated Parmesan cheese

50g salted butter, cold, cut into 1cm cubes

Salt and pepper to taste

FOR THE BÉCHAMEL SAUCE

100g salted butter

100g plain flour

1 litre full-fat milk, cold

¼ nutmeg, freshly grated

1 Heat the olive oil in a large saucepan and cook the onions and celery for 8 minutes on a medium heat. Add in the courgettes, carrots and peppers and continue to cook for a further 10 minutes stirring continuously. Season with salt and pepper.

2 Pour in the wine, stir well and continue to cook for 5 minutes until the alcohol has evaporated. Add the chopped tomatoes, tomato purée and basil, lower the heat and cook for 40 minutes, lid off, until you have a beautiful rich vegetable sauce. Stir occasionally. (After about 20 minutes, taste for seasoning.)

3 To make the béchamel sauce, melt the butter in a large saucepan over a medium heat. Stir in the flour and cook for 1 minute until it turns a light brown colour. Gradually whisk in the cold milk, lower the heat and cook for 10 minutes whisking constantly. Once thickened, stir in the grated nutmeg. Season with salt and pepper and set aside to cool slightly.

4 Preheat the oven to 190°C/gas mark 5.

5 Spread a quarter of the béchamel sauce over the base of a deep-sided 2 litre ovenproof dish. Lay 3 lasagne sheets on top, trimming them if necessary to fit the dish. Spread over half the vegetable sauce then top with a third of the remaining béchamel sauce. Lay 3 more sheets of lasagne on top and cover with the remaining vegetable sauce. Spread over half of the remaining béchamel sauce. Add a final layer of lasagne and gently spread the rest of the béchamel on top. Ensure that the lasagne sheets are completely covered.

6 Sprinkle the top with the Parmesan and scatter over the cubed butter. Grind some black pepper over the whole lasagne.

7 Cover the dish with foil and place in the middle of the oven for 20 minutes then increase the temperature to 200°C/gas mark 6. Remove the foil and continue to cook for a further 20 minutes until golden and crispy all over.

8 Remove the dish from the oven and leave to rest for 10 minutes. This makes it easier to cut and serve as the layers hold together better.

GNOCCHI AL FORNO

Baked potato dumpling with stringy mozzarella cheese

Gnocchi are still not completely appreciated by the British palate and yet everyone who tastes this dish wants the recipe. Potato dumplings with a simple cheese, tomato, basil and onion sauce are truly amazing. If you are having children over for dinner, please try this – they absolutely love it: I haven't served it to a child yet who has not finished the whole plate. For an extra kick, drizzle over a little chilli oil.

Serves 4

4 tablespoons extra virgin olive oil

1 large red onion onion, finely chopped

700ml passata (sieved tomatoes)

10 fresh basil leaves

500g shop-bought plain gnocchi

3 mozzarella balls, drained and cut into 2cm cubes

50g freshly grated Parmesan cheese

Salt and pepper to taste

1 Preheat the oven to 190°C/gas mark 5.

2 Heat the oil in a medium saucepan over a medium heat and fry the onions for 5 minutes. Pour in the sieved tomatoes and cook, uncovered, for 10 minutes. Stir occasionally with a wooden spoon.

3 Stir in the basil, season with salt and pepper and set the pan aside away from the heat.

4 Meanwhile, fill a medium saucepan at least three-quarters full with water. Add in 1 tablespoon of salt and bring to the boil.

5 Cook the gnocchi in the boiling salted water, removing them with a slotted spoon as soon as they start to float to the surface. Drain well and place in the saucepan of cooked tomato sauce. Stir gently together, allowing the sauce to coat the gnocchi evenly. Add in the mozzarella and quickly stir again.

6 Transfer the gnocchi into a large baking dish. Scatter with the Parmesan cheese and bake in the middle of the oven for 10 minutes.

7 Serve hot with a little warm crusty bread.

FUSILLI GRATINATI

Pasta twists with smoked salmon and béchamel sauce

Who says that smoked salmon can only be eaten as a starter or by itself? Trust me: it works beautifully in a baked pasta dish, especially when it's combined with fresh chives, grated Emmental cheese and sweet smoked paprika. A tasty main course that I've often tried when I want to impress and, it's always been successful. Please ensure you buy good-quality smoked salmon and cook the pasta really al dente, otherwise, it will become soggy during the baking. Enjoy!

Serves 6

350g fusilli pasta

80g salted butter, plus extra
   for greasing

200g smoked salmon, cut into
   small strips

4 tablespoons finely chopped
   chives

100g freshly grated Emmental

Salt and pepper to taste

FOR THE BÉCHAMEL SAUCE

50g salted butter

50g plain flour

500ml full-fat milk, cold

Pinch of freshly grated nutmeg

½ teaspoon sweet smoked paprika

1   Grease a 22cm round ovenproof dish with sides at least 5cm deep.

2   To make the béchamel sauce, melt the butter in a large saucepan over a medium heat. Stir in the flour and cook for 1 minute until it turns a light brown colour. Gradually whisk in the cold milk, lower the heat and cook for 10 minutes whisking constantly. Once thickened, stir in the nutmeg and the paprika. Season with salt and pepper and set aside to cool slightly.

3   Fill a large saucepan at least three-quarters full with water. Add in 2 tablespoons of salt and bring to the boil. Cook the pasta in the boiling water until al dente, stirring every minute or so. To get the al dente perfect bite, cook the pasta for 2 minutes less than indicated in the packet instructions.

4   Drain the pasta and tip into a large bowl with the butter, the smoked salmon, chives, half of the Emmental and half of the béchamel sauce. Mix all the ingredients together.

5   Pour the pasta into the ovenproof dish, cover with the remaining béchamel sauce and sprinkle over the remaining cheese.

6   Place the dish under a medium hot grill for 15 minutes until golden and crispy.

7   Remove the dish from the grill and leave to rest for 5 minutes. This makes it easier to cut and serve as the pasta holds together better.

RIGATONI GRATINATI

Rigatoni with aubergines and a crispy Parmesan topping

This is definitely the kind of pasta that ticks all my boxes. The crispiness of a cheesy topping and the sumptuous aubergine and garlic flavours drive me mad. Aubergines in my opinion are not used enough and they happen to be one of my favourite vegetables EVER. What's really great about this pasta dish, is that you can make it in the morning, cover with clingfilm, refrigerate, then cook when ready that night or even the night after. Perfect with a cold bottle of beer.

Serves 6

2 medium aubergines, trimmed

150ml olive oil

4 garlic cloves, peeled and halved

2 x 400g cans cherry tomatoes

10 basil leaves

500g rigatoni

100g freshly grated Parmesan cheese

Salt and pepper to taste

1 Place the aubergines on a chopping board and cut into strips about 1cm wide and 5cm long, discard the centre part containing the seeds.

2 Heat the oil in a large frying pan, add the aubergines and fry for about 5 minutes until golden brown and crispy. Stir occasionally.

3 Use a slotted spoon to remove the aubergines from the pan and drain on kitchen paper. Sprinkle with a little salt.

4 Discard two-thirds of the oil from the pan where you fried the aubergines and fry the garlic in the remaining oil for 30 seconds. Add in the cherry tomatoes with the basil, stir everything together and simmer over a medium heat for 10 minutes. Stir occasionally.

5 Add in the aubergines, stir and continue to cook for a further 5 minutes. Season with salt and pepper and set aside.

6 Fill a large saucepan with 4 litres of water and bring to the boil. Add in 2 tablespoons of salt. Cook the pasta in the boiling water until al dente, stirring every minute or so. To get the al dente perfect bite, cook the pasta for 1 minute less than indicated in the packet instructions. Drain and return the pasta to the same pan.

7 Place the saucepan over a low heat, pour over the aubergine sauce and half the Parmesan cheese. Stir for 30 seconds, allowing all the flavours to combine properly.

8 Transfer to an ovenproof dish large enough to contain all the pasta and sprinkle the top with the remaining Parmesan cheese.

9 Place under a hot grill for 10 minutes until the top is bubbly and crispy.

10 Remove the dish from the grill and leave to rest for 5 minutes before portioning. Enjoy.

CROSTATA DI SPAGHETTI
Spaghetti tart with pine kernels and rocket leaves

Most of my food memories of growing up in Naples consist of some kind of spaghetti dish that my mother would prepare. Today, I still have spaghetti at least once a week with my family and friends and not long ago, I came up with this recipe, which may sound a bit weird but is wonderful and tasty. The richness of the shortcrust pastry with the spinach, cheese, rocket leaves and pasta is a combination made in heaven. If you prefer, substitute the pine kernels with walnuts or the Parmesan cheese with a strong Cheddar.

Serves 8

100g spaghetti

5 tablespoons olive oil

2 red onions, peeled and
   thinly sliced

400g ready-made shortcrust pastry

Plain flour for dusting

150g baby leaf spinach, washed
   and roughly chopped

6 medium eggs

4 tablespoons pine kernels

100g freshly grated Parmesan
   cheese

150g rocket leaves

Salt and pepper to taste

1 Preheat the oven to 180°C/gas mark 4.

2 Fill a large saucepan with 3 litres of water and bring to the boil. Add in 1 tablespoon of salt. Cook the spaghetti in the boiling water until al dente, stirring every minute or so. To get the al dente perfect bite, cook the pasta for 1 minute less than indicated in the packet instructions.

3 Drain the spaghetti in a colander and immediately rinse under cold water to stop the cooking. Once cold, leave on the side to drain for 5 minutes. Give it a good shake every minute.

4 Heat the olive oil in a large frying pan over a medium heat and cook the onions for 5–6 minutes until softened. Stir occasionally and set aside.

5 Roll out the pastry on a lightly floured surface and use to line a 25cm loose-based tart tin. Chill in the freezer for 10 minutes.

6 Line the tart tin with greaseproof paper and fill with baking beans. Place on a baking tray and cook in the middle of the oven for 15 minutes. Take out of the oven, remove the paper and beans and set aside to cool.

7 Meanwhile, blanch the spinach by putting it in a colander over the sink and pouring boiling water over it. Squeeze out the excess water and set aside.

8 Lightly beat the eggs in a large bowl. Add in the pine kernels, cheese, onions, rocket leaves, spinach and spaghetti and season with salt and pepper. Mix all the ingredients together.

9 Pour the mixture into the pastry case, spreading it out evenly.

10 Bake in the middle of the oven for about 30 minutes or until the filling is just set throughout.

11 Allow to cool in the tin for 15 minutes, then remove and transfer to a large plate.

12 Cut into slices and serve warm or at room temperature with a green salad.

PASTICCIO DI PASTA E CARNE
Pasta bake with beef and lamb sauce

I first came across this recipe when I was studying in catering college. It's a typical pasta dish that comes from my home town of Torre del Greco. The meat sauce is fantastic and the cheese creates a creamy texture that everybody will love. Enjoy this with your family instead of the usual Sunday roast and if you fancy, change the lamb mince for pork mince, to give added richness to the sauce.

Serves 6

5 tablespoons olive oil

1 onion, peeled and finely chopped

1 large carrot, peeled and grated

2 celery sticks, finely chopped

500g minced beef

500g minced lamb

100ml red wine

2 x 400g cans chopped tomatoes

2 tablespoons tomato purée

200ml beef stock

Butter for greasing

3 tablespoons toasted fine breadcrumbs

300g fresh tagliatelle or fettuccine

3 mozzarella balls, drained and sliced

70g freshly grated pecorino cheese

Salt and pepper to taste

1   Heat the olive oil in a large saucepan over a medium heat. Fry the onion, carrot and celery for 10 minutes. Stir occasionally with a wooden spoon.

2   Add in the minced meats and continue to cook for a further 5 minutes stirring continuously until coloured all over. Season with salt and pepper.

3   Pour in the wine, stir well and continue to cook for 5 minutes allowing the alcohol to evaporate.

4   Pour in the chopped tomatoes with the tomato purée and the stock, lower the heat and cook for 2 hours with the lid off. Stir the sauce every 15 minutes.

5   Once the sauce is ready, remove from the heat, check the seasoning and set aside.

6   Butter a 30cm round gratin dish (or a rectangular one of about the same size) and sprinkle over the breadcrumbs. Tap off any excess.

7   Preheat the oven to 190°C/gas mark 5.

8   Fill a large saucepan at least three-quarters full with water. Add in 2 tablespoons of salt and bring to the boil. Cook the pasta in the boiling water until al dente, stirring every minute or so. To get the perfect al dente bite, cook the pasta for 1 minute less than indicated in the packet instructions. Drain and return the pasta to the same pan.

9   Pour over the meat sauce and gently stir together for 30 seconds to allow the flavours to combine properly.

10 Spoon half of the pasta mixture into the dish and scatter over the mozzarella cheese. Cover with the remaining pasta.

11 Sprinkle over the pecorino cheese.

12 Bake uncovered in the middle of the oven for 20 minutes.

13 Remove the dish from the oven and leave to rest for 3 minutes before portioning.

ORECCHIETTE CON SALSICCE E BROCCOLETTI

Creamy shells with pork sausages and sprouting broccoli

This is an authentic dish that comes from the region of Puglia in the south of Italy. To be precise it comes from a town called Bari where they are absolutely mad about orecchiette pasta. The translation of the shape of this pasta in English is 'little pretty ears'. If you can't find the orecchiette use any shell pasta. Also, if you really have to, you can substitute the pecorino cheese with Parmesan cheese. However, please, please, please buy good-quality sausages otherwise you will ruin my beautiful pasta dish.

Serves 6

8 tablespoons olive oil

300g sprouting broccoli, cut into 2cm pieces

5 good-quality pork sausages, cut into 1cm pieces

2 garlic cloves, finely sliced

50g walnuts, roughly chopped

1 medium hot red chilli, deseeded and finely sliced

80ml dry white wine

500g orecchiette shells

150g freshly grated pecorino cheese

2 tablespoons freshly chopped flatleaf parsley

250g mascarpone cheese

Salt to taste

1 Preheat the oven to 180°C/gas mark 4.

2 Heat the olive oil in a large frying pan or wok over a medium heat and stir-fry the broccoli, sausages, garlic, walnuts and the chilli for 5 minutes. Stir occasionally with a wooden spoon.

3 Pour in the wine and continue to cook over a medium heat for a further 8 minutes. Ensure that the broccoli stays al dente.

4 Fill a large saucepan with 4 litres of water and bring to the boil. Add in 2 tablespoons of salt. Cook the pasta in the boiling water until al dente, stirring every minute or so. To get the al dente perfect bite, cook the pasta for 1 minute less than indicated in the packet instructions. Drain and return the pasta to the same pan.

5 Pour the broccoli and sausage mixture over the pasta and place the saucepan over a low heat.

6 Sprinkle over half of the pecorino cheese, the parsley and add in the mascarpone. Mix all the ingredients together for 30 seconds to allow the sauce to coat the pasta evenly. At this point please check for seasoning.

7 Transfer the pasta into a large baking dish. Sprinkle over the remaining pecorino cheese and bake in the middle of the oven for 10 minutes.

8 Serve immediately.

PASTICCIO ALLA NAPOLETANA
Neapolitan pasta bake with meatballs

If you run a busy home but love the taste of homemade meat balls and pasta, this recipe is for you. I have created it for that reason. It can be prepared a day in advance and then baked in the oven when ready. A classic Neapolitan pasta dish that has all the ingredients of a masterpiece. You can use pecorino cheese instead of the Parmesan if you prefer and rigatoni pasta would also work for this dish.

Serves 6

10 tablespoons olive oil

1 large white onion, finely chopped

3 x 400g cans chopped tomatoes

10 fresh basil leaves

100g minced lamb

100g minced beef

100g Neapolitan salami, finely chopped

100g freshly made breadcrumbs

5 medium eggs

4 tablespoons plain flour, sprinkled on a flat plate

300g penne rigate

3 mozzarella balls, drained and cut into 2cm chunks

150g freshly grated Parmesan cheese

Salt and pepper to taste

1 First prepare the tomato sauce. Heat 6 tablespoons of olive oil in a medium saucepan over a gentle heat and fry the onions for 5 minutes. Tip in the chopped tomatoes with the fresh basil and leave it to cook over a low heat for 40 minutes without the lid on. Stir every 5 minutes. Once the sauce is ready, season with salt and pepper and set aside.

2 Meanwhile, prepare the meatballs. Put the minced meats in a large bowl with the salami, breadcrumbs and 2 eggs. Season with salt and pepper and mix by squeezing all the ingredients together with one hand. At this point, wet your hands with a little water and roll the meat mixture into balls the size of marbles. Lightly coat the balls in the flour. Heat the remaining oil in a large frying pan over a medium heat and fry the meatballs, turning to seal on all sides. Set aside.

3 Boil the remaining 3 eggs for 7 minutes, drain and leave in the same saucepan under cold water for 5 minutes; this makes it easier to peel them. Shell them and roughly chop them.

4 Preheat the oven to 180°C/gas mark 4.

5 Fill a large saucepan at least three-quarters full with water. Add in 2 tablespoons of salt and bring to the boil. Cook the pasta in the boiling water until very al dente (3 minutes less than instructed on the packet), stirring every minute or so. Drain, rinse under cold water for a minute and then return it to the same pan. Pour over the tomato sauce, add in the meatballs and gently mix all the ingredients together.

6 Pour half of the pasta mixture in a 25 x 32cm lasagne dish. Scatter over half of the mozzarella, half the Parmesan cheese and the boiled eggs. Pour over the rest of the pasta mixture and scatter the top with the remaining mozzarella and Parmesan cheese.

7 Bake in the middle of the oven for 25 minutes until golden brown and bubbling.

8 Remove the dish from the oven and leave to rest for 5 minutes before portioning.

CLASSICA MARGHERITA

Classic pizza with mozzarella, tomatoes and fresh basil

Most babies are weaned off their mother's milk with puréed food, I'm sure my mother weaned us off on pizza as I just don't ever remember life without it. This classic tomato and mozzarella pizza originally was created for the Queen of Naples, Margherita. Never use buffalo mozzarella as it is too milky and will make your pizza base very soggy. Fresh basil is a must: don't you ever attempt to do my pizza with dried basil from a jar, it will ruin a masterpiece! If you like it hot, you can always drizzle a little chilli oil on top before serving.

Makes 2 pizzas

200g strong white flour plus extra for dusting

7g fast-action dried yeast

Pinch of salt

140ml water, warm

3 tablespoons extra virgin olive oil plus extra for brushing

FOR THE TOPPING

200g passata (sieved tomatoes)

2 mozzarella balls, drained and cut into little cubes

4 tablespoons extra virgin olive oil

8 fresh basil leaves

Salt and pepper to taste

1. Prepare 2 baking trays by pouring 1 tablespoon of oil on each tray and spreading it with your fingers or pastry brush. Brush the inside of a large bowl with oil.

2. To prepare the dough, put the flour, yeast and salt into a large bowl, make a well in the centre and pour in the water with 1 tablespoon of oil. Use a wooden spoon to mix everything together to create a wet dough.

3. Turn out the dough onto a well-floured surface and work it with your hands for about 5 minutes until smooth and elastic. Place in the oiled bowl, brush the top with oil and cover with clingfilm. Leave to rest at room temperature for 25 minutes.

4. Preheat the oven to 200°C/gas mark 6.

5. Once rested, turn out the dough onto a well-floured surface and divide it into 2 equal halves. Use your hands to push each one out from the centre, to create 2 round discs about 25cm in diameter. Place the pizza bases on the oiled baking trays.

6. Spread the passata evenly over the top of the bases using the back of a tablespoon. Season with salt and pepper.

7. Divide the mozzarella between the 2 pizzas and drizzle each one with 2 tablespoons of extra virgin olive oil.

8. Cook in the middle of the oven for 18 minutes until golden brown.

9. Two minutes before the end of the cooking, scatter over the basil and continue to cook.

10. Serve hot and enjoy with your favourite cold beer.

CRUDAIOLA

Pizza topped with mozzarella, fresh cherry tomatoes and basil pesto

Crudaiola literally means 'made with raw ingredients'. And this pizza is proof that you can definitely cook a masterpiece with only a few simple ingredients. Fresh cherry tomatoes, mozzarella and basil leaves – a taste of Italy at its best. Traditionally made in my home town, Torre del Greco, and still very popular on every restaurant menu on the Neapolitan coast. Please remember not to use buffalo mozzarella as it will release too much milk and make the pizza soggy.

Makes 2 pizzas

200g strong white flour plus extra
  for dusting

7g fast-action dried yeast

Pinch of salt

140ml water, warm

3 tablespoons extra virgin olive oil
  plus extra for brushing

FOR THE TOPPING

200g cherry tomatoes, quartered

2 mozzarella balls, drained and
  cut into little cubes

3 tablespoons extra virgin olive oil

2 tablespoons basil pesto

Salt and pepper to taste

1   Prepare 2 baking trays by pouring 1 tablespoon of oil on each tray and spread it with your fingers or pastry brush. Brush the inside of a large bowl with oil.

2   To prepare the dough, put the flour, yeast and salt into a large bowl, make a well in the centre and pour in the water with 1 tablespoon of oil. Use a wooden spoon to mix everything together to create a wet dough.

3   Turn out the dough onto a well-floured surface and work it with your hands for about 5 minutes until smooth and elastic. Place in the oiled bowl, brush the top with oil and cover with clingfilm. Leave to rest at room temperature for 25 minutes.

4   Preheat the oven to 200°C/gas mark 6.

5   Place the tomatoes and mozzarella in a large bowl. Pour over the oil and add in the pesto. Season with a little salt and pepper and mix all the ingredients together. Set aside at room temperature for 15 minutes and stir every 5 minutes, allowing all the flavours to combine properly.

6   Once rested, turn out the dough onto a well-floured surface and divide it into 2 equal halves. Use your hands to push each one out from the centre, to create 2 round discs about 25cm in diameter. Place the pizza bases on the oiled baking trays.

7   Divide the tomato and mozzarella mixture between the 2 pizzas and drizzle over any remaining juices left in the bowl.

8   Cook in the middle of the oven for 18 minutes until golden brown.

9   Serve hot and enjoy with your favourite bottle of cold white wine.

VEGETARIANA

Vegetarian pizza topped with peppers, courgettes and red onions

Many vegetarians complain to me that pizza toppings can be a bit boring with the traditional cheese, tomato and perhaps a few mushrooms. We often accompany our meat dishes at home with roasted vegetables so I have basically incorporated those flavours onto a pizza and it works amazingly well. This pizza is so flavoursome and it can also be served as a great vegetarian starter – just cut into thin slices and serve on a bed of rocket leaves. For variation, try it with a few artichokes in oil sliced on top. *Fantastico!*

Makes 2 pizzas

200g strong white flour plus extra for dusting

7g fast-action dried yeast

Pinch of salt

140ml water, warm

3 tablespoons extra virgin olive oil plus extra for brushing

FOR THE TOPPING

4 tablespoons extra virgin olive oil

1 red pepper, trimmed, deseeded and cut into ½cm strips

1 yellow pepper, trimmed, deseeded and cut into ½cm strips

1 large courgette, trimmed and cut into ½cm strips about the length of the pepper strips

1 large red onion, finely sliced

200g passata (sieved tomatoes)

½ teaspoon dried chilli flakes

Salt and pepper to taste

1 Prepare 2 baking trays by pouring 1 tablespoon of oil on each tray and spread it with your fingers or pastry brush. Brush the inside of a large bowl with oil.

2 To prepare the topping, heat the oil in a large frying pan over a medium heat and fry the peppers, courgettes and onions for 10 minutes stirring frequently. Season with salt, leave to cool and set aside.

3 To prepare the dough, put the flour, yeast and salt into a large bowl, make a well in the centre and pour in the water with 1 tablespoon of oil. Use a wooden spoon to mix everything together to create a wet dough.

4 Turn out the dough onto a well-floured surface and work it with your hands for about 5 minutes until smooth and elastic. Place in the oiled bowl, brush the top with oil and cover with clingfilm. Leave to rest at room temperature for 25 minutes.

5 Preheat the oven to 200°C/gas mark 6.

6 Once rested, turn out the dough onto a well-floured surface and divide it into 2 equal halves. Use your hands to push each one out from the centre, to create 2 round discs about 25cm in diameter. Place the pizza bases on the oiled baking trays.

8 Spread the passata evenly over the top of the bases using the back of a tablespoon. Season with salt and pepper.

9 Scatter the cooked vegetables over the 2 pizzas.

10 Cook in the middle of the oven for 18 minutes until golden.

11 Two minutes before the end of the cooking, sprinkle over the chilli flakes and continue to cook.

12 Serve hot and enjoy.

LA FIORENTINA

Pizza topped with mozzarella, spinach, egg and Parmesan cheese

A masterpiece from the city of Florence and if you are craving pizza with lots of healthy protein, this is the one for you. You can't get a more nutritious pizza. The kids love it as it's another way of serving them fried eggs but with a twist and getting them to eat green veg is always a winner. This one is a firm favourite in the D'Acampo house and invariably leads to arguments over who gets the last piece.

Makes 2 pizzas

200g strong white flour plus extra for dusting

7g fast-action dried yeast

Pinch of salt

140ml water, warm

3 tablespoons extra virgin olive oil plus extra for brushing

FOR THE TOPPING

4 tablespoons extra virgin olive oil

300g frozen spinach, defrosted

2 mozzarella balls, drained and cut into little cubes

2 large eggs

4 tablespoons freshly grated Parmesan cheese

Salt and pepper to taste

1 Prepare 2 baking trays by pouring 1 tablespoon of oil in each tray and spread it with your fingers or pastry brush. Brush the inside of a large bowl with oil.

2 To prepare the dough, put the flour, yeast and salt into a large bowl, make a well in the centre and pour in the water with 1 tablespoon of oil. Use a wooden spoon to mix everything together to create a wet dough.

3 Turn out the dough onto a well-floured surface and work it with your hands for about 5 minutes until smooth and elastic. Place in the oiled bowl, brush the top with oil and cover with clingfilm. Leave to rest at room temperature for 25 minutes.

4 Preheat the oven to 200°C/gas mark 6.

5 Squeeze the spinach between your hands, allowing any excess water to drain away. Set aside.

6 Once rested, turn out the dough onto a well-floured surface and divide it into 2 equal halves. Use your hands to push each one out from the centre, to create 2 round discs about 25cm in diameter. Place the pizza bases on the oiled baking trays. Brush the bases with oil.

7 Divide the mozzarella between the 2 pizzas and scatter over the spinach. but leave an empty circle of about 5cm diameter in the centre of both pizzas because this is where the egg will eventually be placed.

8 Cook in the middle of the oven for 8 minutes. Remove the pizzas from the oven, crack an egg into the empty circle at the centre of each pizza and return them to the oven to cook for a further 10 minutes.

9 Two minutes before the end of the cooking, scatter over the Parmesan.

10 Serve and enjoy hot.

PIZZA VOLANTE

Pizza stuffed with mozzarella, ricotta and spinach

I absolutely adore this pizza and if you like pizza half as much as me you too will love this one! Envisage a pizza sandwich – it doesn't get much better than that! This one can even be eaten cold on a picnic or for a packed lunch and of course you can pretty much come up with any fillings that you wish, although I love the flavour of the spinach with the cheese and the crunchiness of the pine kernels. Perfect for any occasion and so easy to make – you will hardly ever order a pizza take-away again!

Makes 1 disc/serves 2

200g strong white flour plus extra for dusting

7g fast-action dried yeast

Pinch of salt

140ml water, warm

3 tablespoons extra virgin olive oil plus extra for brushing

FOR THE STUFFING

200g ricotta cheese

¼ grated nutmeg

1 mozzarella ball, drained and cut into little cubes

100g frozen spinach, defrosted, squeeze any excess water

3 tablespoons pine kernels

Salt and pepper to taste

1 Brush a large baking tray and the inside of a large bowl with oil.

2 To prepare the dough, put the flour, yeast and salt into a large bowl, make a well in the centre and pour in the water with 1 tablespoon of oil. Use a wooden spoon to mix everything together to create a wet dough.

3 Turn out the dough onto a well-floured surface and work it with your hands for about 5 minutes or until smooth and elastic. Place in the oiled bowl, brush the top with a little oil and cover with clingfilm. Leave to rest at room temperature for 25 minutes.

4 Preheat the oven to 200°C/gas mark 6.

5 Once rested, turn out the dough onto a well-floured surface and divide it into 2 equal halves. Use your hands to push each one out from the centre, to create 2 round discs about 20cm in diameter.

6 Place 1 disc on the oiled baking tray. Spread the ricotta cheese on top of the pizza using the back of a tablespoon, season with salt and pepper and sprinkle with nutmeg. Scatter over the mozzarella, spinach and pine kernels.

7 Gently lift the second disc and place it on top of the filled one. Bring the edges together to enclose the filling. Pinch to seal and turn over the edges to create a rope-like effect.

8 Brush the surface of the filled pizza disc with oil.

9 Cook in the middle of the oven for 18 minutes, until golden brown.

10 Serve hot and share with your loved ones.

CALZONE NAPOLETANO

Traditional Neapolitan folded pizza stuffed with mozzarella, ham and mushrooms

Every time I go to Naples and I'm out with my father Ciro, he will only ever order the same pizza – and this is it. (Calzone, incidentally, means a pair of trousers, a connection which I've never understood.) You can stuff this folded pizza with anything you fancy but whatever you choose, please ensure that the edges are sealed properly, otherwise you will end up with a big mess in the oven. Perfect with a cold Italian beer.

Makes 2 pizzas

200g strong white flour

7g fast-action dried yeast

Pinch of salt

140ml water, warm

3 tablespoons extra virgin olive oil plus extra for brushing

FOR THE STUFFING

2 tablespoons extra virgin olive oil

100g chestnut mushrooms, sliced

150g passata (sieved tomatoes)

2 mozzarella balls, cubed small

100g sliced cooked ham, diced

Salt and pepper to taste

1 Prepare 2 baking trays by pouring 1 tablespoon of oil in each tray and spread it with your fingers or pastry brush. Brush the inside of a large bowl with oil.

2 To prepare the dough, put the flour, yeast and salt into a large bowl, make a well in the centre and pour in the water with 1 tablespoon of oil. Use a wooden spoon to mix everything together to create a wet dough.

3 Turn out the dough onto a well-floured surface and work it with your hands for about 5 minutes or until smooth and elastic. Place in the oiled bowl, brush the top with a little oil and cover with clingfilm. Leave to rest at room temperature for 25 minutes.

4 Preheat the oven to 200°C/gas mark 6.

5 Heat 2 tablespoons of oil in a large frying pan over a medium heat and gently fry the mushrooms for 5 minutes. Stir occasionally and season with a little salt at the end. Allow to cool.

6 Once rested, turn out the dough onto a well-floured surface and divide it into 2 equal halves. Use your hands to push each one out from the centre, to create 2 round discs about 25cm in diameter. Place the pizza bases on the oiled baking trays.

7 Spread the passata evenly over just half the surface of both pizza discs using the back of a tablespoon. Season with salt and pepper.

8 Divide the mozzarella, mushrooms and cooked ham between the 2 pizzas; at this point you should have half of each pizza complete with topping and the other half empty.

9 Bring over the edge of the unfilled half to cover and enclose the filling. Pinch to seal and turn over the edges to create a rope-like effect.

10 Cook in the middle of the oven for 18 minutes, until golden brown.

11 Serve hot and enjoy with your favourite salad.

FOCACCIA ALLA CAPRICCIOSA
Large focaccia topped with ham, mushrooms, garlic and olives

Many of my friends like a thicker crust on their pizza so I came up with a solution for them. The focaccia has a flavour in its own right and topping it with cheese, garlic, ham and mushrooms makes this simple-tasting bread the ultimate thick crust pizza. Perfect for a starter, great in a packed lunch, delicious if you are watching a movie, I've even been known to eat it cold for breakfast after a heavy night – *fantastico* any time.

Serves 10

500g strong white flour plus extra
  for dusting

7g fast-action dried yeast

3 tablespoons extra virgin olive oil
  plus extra for brushing

300ml warm water

2 teaspoons fine salt

FOR THE TOPPING

2 mozzarella balls, drained and
  cut into 1cm cubes

200g sliced cooked ham,
  cut into strips

100g button mushrooms,
  finely sliced

2 garlic cloves, peeled and
  crushed

50g pitted green olives,
  quartered

3 tablespoons extra virgin
  olive oil

300g passata (sieved tomatoes)

Salt and pepper to taste

1   Brush a large baking tray and the inside of a large bowl with oil.

2   Sift the flour into a large bowl and stir in the yeast. Make a well in the centre and pour in the oil with the water. Add the salt and with the help of a wooden spoon, mix together until all the ingredients are well combined.

3   Transfer the mixture onto a lightly floured surface and knead for 10 minutes until you have a smooth and elastic dough. The dough should be soft and if it is really sticky add a little more flour.

4   Fold the edges of the dough underneath to create a smooth rounded ball. Place the dough into the oiled bowl and brush the top with oil to prevent a crust from forming. Cover with clingfilm and leave to rise in a warm place away from draughts for 1 hour until doubled in size.

5   Slide the dough onto the oiled baking tray. Press with your fingertips to make indentations in the dough, flattening it into an oval shape about 3cm thick. Brush with a little oil and cover with clingfilm. Leave it to rise in a warm place away from draughts for 40 minutes.

6   Preheat the oven to 220°C/gas mark 7.

7   Put the mozzarella, ham, mushrooms, garlic and olives in a large bowl. Pour over the oil and season with a little salt and pepper. Mix all the ingredients together and set aside at room temperature for 15 minutes. Stir every 5 minutes, allowing all the flavours to combine properly.

8   Once the dough has risen, use your fingertips again to press more indentations into the dough. Spread over the passata to within 1cm of the edges. Scatter over the mozzarella and ham mixture.

9   Bake in the middle of the oven for 20 minutes until golden and beautiful. Slide the focaccia off the baking tray and allow to cool slightly on a wire rack so that it does not sweat underneath.

10 Cut into 10 slices and serve warm.

DIAVOLETTO
The ultimate spicy pizza

Diavoletto means 'little devil' in Italian. Whenever I go out with the boys for a pizza there are a few who insist on drowning theirs with chilli olive oil. They love the strong spicy flavour so I wanted to create the ultimate spicy pizza and here it is. No one will ever add chilli oil to this one! I have only used red ingredients so it looks as good as tastes: HOT! Perfect with a beer ... or four.

Makes 2 pizzas

200g strong white flour plus extra
    for dusting

7g fast-action dried yeast

Pinch of salt

140ml water, warm

3 tablespoons extra virgin olive oil
    plus extra for brushing

FOR THE TOPPING

4 tablespoons extra virgin olive oil

1 red pepper, deseeded and cut
    into ½cm strips

1 fresh red chilli, deseeded and
    finely chopped

1 large red onion, finely sliced

200g passata (sieved tomatoes)

1 teaspoons dried chilli flakes

2 mozzarella balls, drained and
    cut into 1cm cubes

20 slices Milano salami

Salt and pepper to taste

1 Prepare 2 baking trays by pouring 1 tablespoon of oil in each tray and spread it with your fingers or pastry brush. Brush the inside of a large bowl with oil.

2 To prepare the topping, heat the oil in a large frying pan over a medium heat and fry the peppers, chilli and onions for 8 minutes stirring frequently. Season with salt, leave to cool and set aside.

3 To prepare the dough, put the flour, yeast and salt into a large bowl, make a well in the centre and pour in the water with 1 tablespoon of oil. Use a wooden spoon to mix everything together to create a wet dough.

4 Turn out the dough onto a well-floured surface and work it with your hands for about 5 minutes until smooth and elastic. Place in the oiled bowl, brush the top with oil and cover with clingfilm. Leave to rest at room temperature for 25 minutes.

5 Preheat the oven to 200°C/gas mark 6.

6 Once rested, turn out the dough onto a well-floured surface and divide it into 2 equal halves. Use your hands to push each one out from the centre, to create 2 round discs about 25cm in diameter. Place the pizza bases on the oiled baking trays.

7 Spread the passata evenly over the top of the bases using the back of a tablespoon. Sprinkle over the chilli flakes and season with salt and pepper.

8 Scatter the mozzarella and cooked vegetables over the 2 pizzas and divide the salami on top.

9 Cook in the middle of the oven for 18 minutes until golden brown.

10 Serve hot and enjoy with a cold beer.

PIZZA VOLANTE AI SALUMI
Pizza stuffed with mascarpone, salami Milano, bresaola and Parma ham

Meat, meat and more meat – I love this pizza. The use of three different hams with cheese is delicious. Making that first cut into the pizza and enjoying all the flavours oozing out is worth any amount of time you spent preparing it. Picture after a hard day's work eating this dish with a large glass of red wine – it's the perfect ending to any day. If you prefer, add in mozzarella to get that extra gooey cheesy flavour.

Makes 1 disc/serves 2

200g strong white flour plus extra for dusting

7g fast-action dried yeast

Pinch of salt

140ml water, warm

3 tablespoons extra virgin olive oil plus extra for brushing

FOR THE STUFFING

200g mascarpone cheese, at room temperature

8 slices salami Milano

6 slices Parma ham

8 slices bresaola

Salt and pepper to taste

1   Brush a large baking tray and the inside of a large bowl with oil.

2   To prepare the dough, put the flour, yeast and salt into a large bowl, make a well in the centre and pour in the water with 1 tablespoon of oil. Use a wooden spoon to mix everything together to create a wet dough.

3   Turn out the dough onto a well-floured surface and work it with your hands for about 5 minutes or until smooth and elastic. Place in the oiled bowl, brush the top with a little oil and cover with clingfilm. Leave to rest at room temperature for 25 minutes.

4   Preheat the oven to 200°C/gas mark 6.

5   Once rested, turn out the dough onto a well-floured surface and divide it into two equal halves. Use your hands to push each one out from the centre, to create 2 round discs about 20cm in diameter.

6   Place 1 disc on the oiled baking tray. Spread the mascarpone cheese on top of the pizza using the back of a tablespoon, and season with salt and pepper. Top with the salami, bresaola and Parma ham, distributing the meats evenly.

7   Gently lift the second disc and place it on top of the filled one. Bring together the edges to enclose the filling. Pinch to seal and turn over the edges to create a rope-like effect.

8   Brush the surface of the filled pizza disc with oil.

9   Cook in the middle of the oven for 18 minutes, until golden brown.

10 Serve hot with a big glass of Italian dry red wine.

QUATTRO STAGIONI

Four seasons pizza topped with ham, artichokes, mushrooms and olives

Globe artichokes are used a lot in Europe, and especially in Italy, but don't seem to be very popular here in England. However, artichoke hearts are essential on this pizza as they work beautifully with the ham, mushrooms and olives. I have tried making this recipe with rocket leaves instead of the mushrooms and it's just as good. A classic Italian four seasons pizza that just reminds me of home.

Makes 2 pizzas

200g strong white flour plus extra
    for dusting

7g fast-action dried yeast

Pinch of salt

140ml water, warm

3 tablespoons extra virgin olive oil
    plus extra for brushing

FOR THE TOPPING

2 tablespoons extra virgin olive oil

80g chestnut mushrooms, sliced

200g passata (sieved tomatoes)

2 mozzarella balls, drained and cut
    into small cubes

100g pitted Kalamata olives,
    quartered

80g sliced cooked ham, cut
    into strips

6 artichokes hearts in oil, drained
    and quartered

Salt and pepper to taste

1 Prepare 2 baking trays by pouring 1 tablespoon of oil in each tray and spread it with your fingers or pastry brush. Brush the inside of a large bowl with oil.

2 To prepare the topping, heat the oil in a large frying pan over a high heat, and fry the mushrooms for 5 minutes stirring frequently. Season with salt, leave to cool and set aside.

3 To prepare the dough, place the flour, yeast and salt into a large bowl, make a well in the centre and pour in the water with 1 tablespoon of oil. Use a wooden spoon to mix everything together to create a wet dough.

4 Turn out the dough onto a well-floured surface and work it with your hands for about 5 minutes or until smooth and elastic. Place in the oiled bowl, brush the top with oil and cover with clingfilm. Leave to rest at room temperature for 25 minutes.

5 Preheat the oven to 200°C/gas mark 6.

6 Once rested, turn out the dough onto a well-floured surface. Roll 4 little pieces of dough into 22cm-long strings, and set them aside. Divide the remaining dough into two equal halves. Use your hands to push each one out from the centre to create 2 discs about 22cm in diameter. Gently lift the pizza bases onto the oiled baking trays.

7 Spread the passata evenly over the bases using the back of a tablespoon and season with salt and pepper. Scatter the mozzarella cheese on top.

8 Use 2 dough strings per pizza to make a cross on top of each. Press the ends of the strings onto the edge of the base to secure. Both pizzas will have 4 triangle shapes. Fill one triangle with olives, one with ham, the next with artichokes and the last with mushrooms.

9 Cook in the middle of the oven for 18 minutes until golden brown.

10 Serve hot and enjoy.

PARTY

GRISSINI AL PARMIGIANO
Classic Italian breadsticks

How cool would it be to bake your own grissini sticks ... well here it is, the easiest recipe in the book and yet one of the most impressive. For me, this is the perfect way to start a dinner party and I promise you, these taste so great no one will believe that you actually made them. You can even prepare them in the morning leaving yourself free to organise your menu. Once the breadsticks are cold, simply wrap a slice of Parma ham around each one and place them on a large serving plate – try it, you will not be disappointed. Enjoy!

Makes about 30 grissini

330g strong white flour plus extra for dusting

7g fast-action dried yeast

200ml full-fat milk, warm

100g freshly grated Parmesan cheese

100g salted soft butter plus extra for greasing

2 pinches of salt

2 pinches of freshly ground black pepper

1 Lightly grease a baking tray and preheat the oven to 160°C/ gas mark 3.

2 Mix the yeast and milk together in a medium bowl.

3 Mix the remaining ingredients together in a large bowl. Pour over the milk with the dissolved yeast and use your fingers to form a dough.

4 Transfer the dough to a lightly floured surface and roll out to a 5mm thickness.

5 Cut into lengths about 40cm long and 1cm wide.

6 Transfer the grissini onto the greased baking tray and cook in the middle of the oven for about 27 minutes until golden brown.

7 Serve warm or allow them to cool on a wire rack and then wrap each breadstick with a slice of Parma ham.

FUNGHI RIPIENI PICCANTI

Spicy stuffed mushrooms with chilli, pine kernels and fresh mint

I love to make this when I want something quick and very tasty. It's also a great vegetarian starter that can be prepared ahead and cooked when needed. If you want, substitute the pecorino cheese with Parmesan cheese and try using walnuts instead of pine kernels for a deeper flavour. Do ensure your mushrooms are firm and please never use dried mint as that would ruin the whole dish.

Serves 10

10 large field mushrooms

1 teaspoon dried chilli flakes

2 tablespoons finely chopped
    fresh mint

3 tablespoons finely chopped
    flatleaf parsley

2 tablespoons pine kernels,
    chopped

50g freshly grated pecorino cheese

5 tablespoons freshly made
    breadcrumbs

2 garlic cloves, finely chopped
    or crushed

130ml extra virgin olive oil

Salt and pepper to taste

1. Preheat the oven to 180°C/gas mark 4.

2. Gently remove the stalks from the mushrooms, put the stalks on a board and chop into small pieces. Tip them into a large bowl with the rest of the ingredients. Season with salt and pepper and mix everything together.

3. Place the mushrooms, gills facing upwards, on a baking tray.

4. Spoon the filling into the cavity of each mushroom and pack it down with the back of the spoon.

5. Bake in the middle of the oven for 15 minutes.

6. Transfer the mushrooms to a large plate and serve as a starter, hot or warm, with some warm crusty bread.

TORTA DI POLLO E VERDURE
Chicken and vegetable pie with lemon zest

This recipe comes from a town called Pompei, not far away from the place where I was born in the south of Italy. The lemons that grow there are unbelievable and my mother always used to make this pie for me and my sister Marcella at least once a week. I've tried many times to change the dish by adding more ingredients but you know what ... my mother's version is the best. If you want, though, you can use turkey in place of chicken or even make the pie vegetarian by substituting the meat with aubergines.

Serves 8

10 tablespoons olive oil plus extra for oiling

1 large red onion, finely sliced

1 tablespoon rosemary leaves, finely chopped

1 yellow pepper, trimmed, deseeded and cut into 2cm cubes

1 leek, trimmed, cut lengthways then finely sliced

1 courgette, trimmed, cut lengthways then sliced 1cm thick

2 skinless, boneless chicken breasts, cut into 3cm cubes

4 tablespoons plain flour

2 medium eggs

70g grated Parmesan cheese

Zest of 1 unwaxed lemon

100ml double cream

2 sheets ready-rolled puff pastry

Salt and pepper to taste

1 Brush a 25cm fluted, loose-based, flan tin with oil and preheat the oven to 180°C/gas mark 4.

2 Pour 5 tablespoons of oil into a large frying pan over a medium heat and start to fry the onion for 2 minutes. Add in the rosemary with the rest of the vegetables, season with salt and pepper and continue to cook for a further 8 minutes stirring occasionally. Remove everything from the pan with a slotted spoon and set aside.

4 Place the chicken pieces in a large bowl and tip in the flour. Coat the chicken evenly, tap off any excess flour, and set aside.

5 Pour the remaining oil into the same frying pan used to cook the vegetables and fry the chicken pieces until golden and brown on all sides. Set aside with the vegetables.

6 Whisk together 1 egg, the Parmesan cheese, lemon zest and cream. Season with salt and pepper.

7 Line the base of the flan tin with one sheet of the ready-rolled puff pastry and arrange the vegetables and the chicken on top. Pour over the egg mixture and cover with the remaining pastry sheet. Pinch the edges together to secure and trim if necessary.

8 Beat the remaining egg in a bowl and brush over the pie. Make a little cut in the centre of the pastry to allow the steam to escape.

9 Bake in the middle of the oven for 30 minutes until beautiful and golden.

10 Remove from the oven and allow the pie to rest for 2 minutes before unmoulding – it will then be easier to cut into slices.

11 Serve warm accompanied with a mixed salad of your choice.

TORTA RIPIENA SALATA

Stuffed savoury cake with cooked ham, sun-dried tomatoes and Taleggio cheese

If one of your favourite sandwich options is ham, cheese and tomato, then this is definitely a recipe for you. It is the ultimate party snack and your guests will just love it. Instead of Taleggio you can also use pretty much any blue cheese of your choice but do try to keep the spinach in; it really gives the cake a lovely texture and colour. Perfect for a picnic party with a cold beer.

Serves 6

450g strong white flour

2 teaspoons dried yeast

4 tablespoons extra virgin olive oil, plus extra for brushing

300ml water, warm

300g frozen spinach, defrosted

200g Taleggio cheese, cut into cubes

150g sun-dried tomatoes in oil, drained and sliced into strips

2 teaspoons fresh thyme leaves

Salt and pepper to taste

100g sliced cooked ham

Sea salt for sprinkling

1 Brush a 25cm loose-based cake tin and the inside of a large bowl with oil.

2 Sift the flour into a large bowl and stir in the yeast. Make a well in the centre, pour in the oil and the water and with the help of a wooden spoon, mix all the ingredients together.

3 Transfer the mixture to a floured surface and knead for 10 minutes until you have a smooth and elastic dough.

4 Place the dough in the oiled bowl, cover with clingfilm and leave to rise in a warm place away from draughts for about 1½ hours until doubled in size.

5 Preheat the oven to 220°C/gas mark 7.

6 Squeeze the spinach to remove any excess water and place in another large bowl. Add in the Taleggio cheese, the sun-dried tomatoes and the thyme. Season with salt and pepper and mix well.

7 Punch down the dough and divide equally into two pieces. Roll out the first piece a little larger than the tin. Place on the base of the tin and try to mould the sides higher than the base.

8 Spread the spinach mixture over the base to within 1cm of the edges. Cover the spinach mixture with the sliced ham.

9 Roll out the remaining dough to the same size as the tin, brush the edges with a little water and place over the filling. Press the edges together really well to ensure a good seal.

10 Gently press your fingertips into the dough to make indentations then brush with extra virgin olive oil. Sprinkle with the sea salt and bake in the middle of the oven for 30 minutes until risen and firm.

11 Remove from the oven and leave to rest into the tin for 10 minutes on a wire rack allowing the air to circulate all around it.

12 Serve and enjoy while still warm and fragrant.

CROSTATA DI FRAGOLE E MANDORLE

Strawberry and almond tart with pistachio topping

When I first came to this country my mother-in-law, Elizabeth, always used to have small Bakewell tarts in the cupboard – it was love at first taste. The combination of almonds, icing, jam and pastry is amazing and instead of feeling guilty because I'd eaten three or more at a time, I decided to make a big one and then the slicing would be down to me. This is such an easy tart to make and it's good made with either strawberry or raspberry jam. Perfect served at room temperature with a cup of tea or coffee!

Serves 8

375g ready-made sweetcrust pastry

5 tablespoons good-quality strawberry jam

125g caster sugar

50g salted butter, at room temperature

3 medium eggs, beaten

125g ground almonds

1 teaspoon almond extract

250g icing sugar

100g crushed pistachio nuts

4 tablespoons water

1 Preheat the oven to 200°C/gas mark 6.

2 Roll out the pastry and use to line a 23cm, loose-based flan tin. Using the back of a fork mark the rim. Spread the jam over the base and place the flan tin in the fridge.

3 Beat the sugar, butter, eggs, ground almonds and almond extract together in a large bowl. Remove the tart case from the fridge, pour the filling over the jam and spread evenly.

4 Bake in the middle of the oven for 30 minutes. Remove from the oven and allow to cool slightly.

5 Sift the icing sugar into a small clean bowl. Stir in the pistachio nuts, pour in the water and mix well (add a little more if it is too thick). Pour the lot into the centre of the tart and spread evenly right to the edges.

6 Serve warm or at room temperature with a cup of tea.

DOLCETTI CON FRAGOLE ED ACETO BALSAMICO

Italian-style scones with strawberries and balsamic vinegar

Seventeen years ago, within the first couple of months of my being in England, I had my first-ever English cream tea and was in heaven. I have often made scones for friends and family and have many variations, but this has to be one of my favourites. The scones are perfected with a touch of amaretto liqueur and the jam has that unexpected kick that just work deliciously together. I prefer to eat my scones slightly warm with a good cup of breakfast tea. Yummy!

Makes 8

225g self-raising flour
Pinch of salt
1 teaspoon baking powder
40g unsalted butter
50ml amaretto liqueur
100ml full-fat milk

FOR THE FILLING

4 tablespoons strawberry jam
100g fresh strawberries, hulled
  and quartered
2 tablespoons balsamic vinegar
250g clotted cream

1 Lightly grease a baking sheet and preheat the oven to 220°C/gas mark 7.

2 Place the jam with the strawberries in a medium saucepan. Pour in the balsamic vinegar and cook over a low heat for 5 minutes. Stir occasionally then set aside and leave to cool.

3 Sift the flour, salt and baking powder into a large bowl. Add the butter and rub in with your fingertips until the mixture resembles fine crumbs. Pour in the amaretto liqueur and stir in enough milk to form a fairly soft, light dough.

4 Transfer the dough to a lightly floured surface and gently roll out to a thickness of 2cm and then cut into rounds using a 6cm plain cutter. (Do not twist the cutter as you lift it from the dough otherwise the scones will not rise properly). Gather up the trimmings and re-roll the dough to give you a total of 8 scones.

5 Gently place the scones on the baking sheet, spaced well apart, and bake in the middle of the oven for 10 minutes until golden brown and well risen.

6 Remove the sheet from the oven and transfer the scones to a wire rack to cool.

7 Serve warm with clotted cream and the balsamic strawberries.

PANNA COTTA
Panna cotta with amaretto

If you love Italian food, especially desserts, you must learn how to make a good panna cotta. Every dinner party should definitely end with this simple but delicious dessert – double cream and amaretto liqueur is a marriage made in heaven. If you find your panna cotta is a little too soft, the next time you make it add an extra gelatine leaf, that will do the trick. For variation, try using limoncello or even Grand Marnier in place of the amaretto. *Buonissimo!*

Serves 6

1.2 litres double cream
Zest of 2 unwaxed oranges
140g caster sugar
2 teaspoons vanilla extract
120ml skimmed milk
4 gelatine leaves
80ml amaretto liqueur

1 Pour 800ml of the cream into a saucepan with the orange zest, caster sugar and vanilla extract. Bring to the boil then simmer until the mixture is reduced by a third.

2 Meanwhile, pour the milk into a small saucepan and soak the gelatine leaves for 5 minutes in the cold milk. After this time, remove the leaves and reserve on a plate. Place the pan with the milk over a low heat and gently warm it through. Once ready, return the gelatine to the milk and stir to dissolve.

3 Stir the milk into the warm cream mixture, pass through a sieve into a large bowl and leave to cool.

4 Lightly whip the remaining cream in another large bowl and gently fold into the setting mixture, together with the amaretto liqueur.

5 Pour the cooled mixture into 6 dariole moulds and place in the fridge to set for at least 4 hours.

6 To serve, remove the panna cotta from the fridge and run a knife around the edges to loosen. Place a serving plate over the top and invert.

7 Remove the moulds and enjoy the panna cotta accompanied with fresh fruits all around it.

TORTA DI CILIEGIE
Cherry and Grand Marnier pudding

I love cherries but there aren't many recipes that use them, so I set myself a challenge and came up with this wonderful pudding. The creamy texture of the custard with the marinated cherries is a match made in heaven. If you are using canned cherries, ensure you drain them very well otherwise the juice will leak into the batter and make it too soggy. Instead of pitted cherries you can use make this with raspberries, blueberries or blackberries or a mixture of them all.

Serves 8

400g fresh pitted cherries or
    canned pitted cherries (drained)
4 tablespoons Grand Marnier

FOR THE BATTER
60g plain flour
90g caster sugar
25g unsalted butter, melted, plus
    extra for brushing
250ml full-fat milk
4 medium eggs, lightly beaten
Icing sugar for dusting

1 Brush a 23cm-diameter ceramic shallow dish with a little melted butter. Preheat the oven to 180°C/gas mark 4.

2 Place the cherries in a glass bowl, pour over the Grand Marnier and leave to marinate for at least 15 minutes.

3 Sift the flour into a large bowl and add in the sugar. Gradually pour in the butter, milk and eggs and whisk until smooth.

4 Place the marinated cherries into the dish and pour over the batter. With the help of a tablespoon, spread the mixture evenly in the dish.

5 Bake in the middle of the oven for 30–35 minutes.

6 Remove the pudding from the oven and leave it rest for 5 minutes.

7 Dust with icing sugar and serve immediately with a little clotted cream.

SFORMATO DOLCE AL CAFFE
Coffee and vanilla brownies

There are so many recipes for brownies but this is one of the easiest you will ever try. I have added coffee to give it a little kick but really anything goes. If you fancy being a bit more experimental you can add in a little brandy or for something a little crunchier, try adding in some crushed hazelnuts and marshmallow pieces – all such concoctions are *fantastico*. If you want to serve these as a dessert, use a biscuit cutter to create a shape of your choosing and top with some fresh berries and vanilla ice cream. Do ensure you use vanilla extract as its flavour is much better than the essence.

Serves 6

125g dark chocolate, at least 70% cocoa solids, broken into chunks

150g unsalted butter plus extra for greasing

3 eggs

1 teaspoon vanilla extract

375g caster sugar

30g cocoa powder

2 tablespoons instant coffee powder

125g plain flour, sifted

1 Grease a 20 x 24cm baking tin (the sides should be at least 5cm deep) with butter and line with greaseproof paper, allowing the paper to extend above the height of sides. Preheat the oven to 180°C/gas mark 4.

2 Place the chocolate and butter into a small glass bowl over a pan of simmering water and allow to melt (ensure the bowl does not touch the water otherwise the chocolate will become bitter). Continue stirring until everything has melted and is smooth. Remove from the heat and leave to cool.

3 Whisk together the eggs, vanilla and sugar in a large bowl. Add in the cooled chocolate mixture then stir in the cocoa, coffee powder and flour.

4 Pour the mixture into the prepared tin and cook in the middle of the oven for 40 minutes.

5 Remove from the oven and leave to cool in the tin for 10 minutes, then lift the brownie out of the tin and onto a chopping board. Cut into slices or shapes.

6 Serve warm with your favourite ice cream or at room temperature with a cup of coffee.

SOUFFLÉS AL CIOCCOLATO CON SALSA DI LAMPONI

Hot chocolate soufflés with raspberry and amaretto sauce

You are probably looking at this recipe right now and thinking OMG, I will never be able to do that. Well, you are wrong because this has to be the easiest soufflé ever created and once you have poured yourself a glass of wine to relax, it's going to be a walk in the park. You can happily make the sauce with strawberries or blackberries instead of raspberries.

Serves 6

300g dark chocolate, at least 70% cocoa solids

4 egg yolks

8 egg whites

30g salted butter, room temperature, plus extra for greasing

120g caster sugar, plus extra for dusting

FOR THE SAUCE

250g raspberries

70g icing sugar plus extra for dusting

100ml amaretto liqueur

1 Butter 6 individual tall-sided ramekins, sprinkle with caster sugar inside and shake off any excess. Chill until required. Preheat the oven to 220°C/gas mark 7.

2 Melt the chocolate in a small glass bowl over a pan of simmering water and allow to melt (ensure the bowl does not touch the water otherwise the chocolate will become bitter). Beat in the 4 egg yolks, one at the time, until the mixture thickens.

3 In a large, spotlessly clean, bowl, whisk the egg whites until stiff. Whisk in the caster sugar, one tablespoon at a time.

4 Fold a little of the meringue into the melted chocolate, then fold the chocolate mix into the remaining meringue until evenly combined.

5 Divide the soufflé mixture between the prepared ramekins. Run a clean finger between the inside edge of each ramekin and the mixture to form a small groove. This will help the soufflés to rise evenly.

6 Place the ramekins on a baking tray and bake in the middle of the oven for 14 minutes until well risen and just wobbly in the middle.

7 Meanwhile, make the sauce. Blitz the raspberries in a food processor or with a stick blender then pass through a sieve into a small saucepan.

8 Add in the icing sugar and the Amaretto liqueur. Bring to a simmer and cook for 5 minutes until slightly reduced. Stir occasionally.

9 As soon as the soufflés are cooked, dust with icing sugar and serve immediately with the warm raspberry sauce.

Index

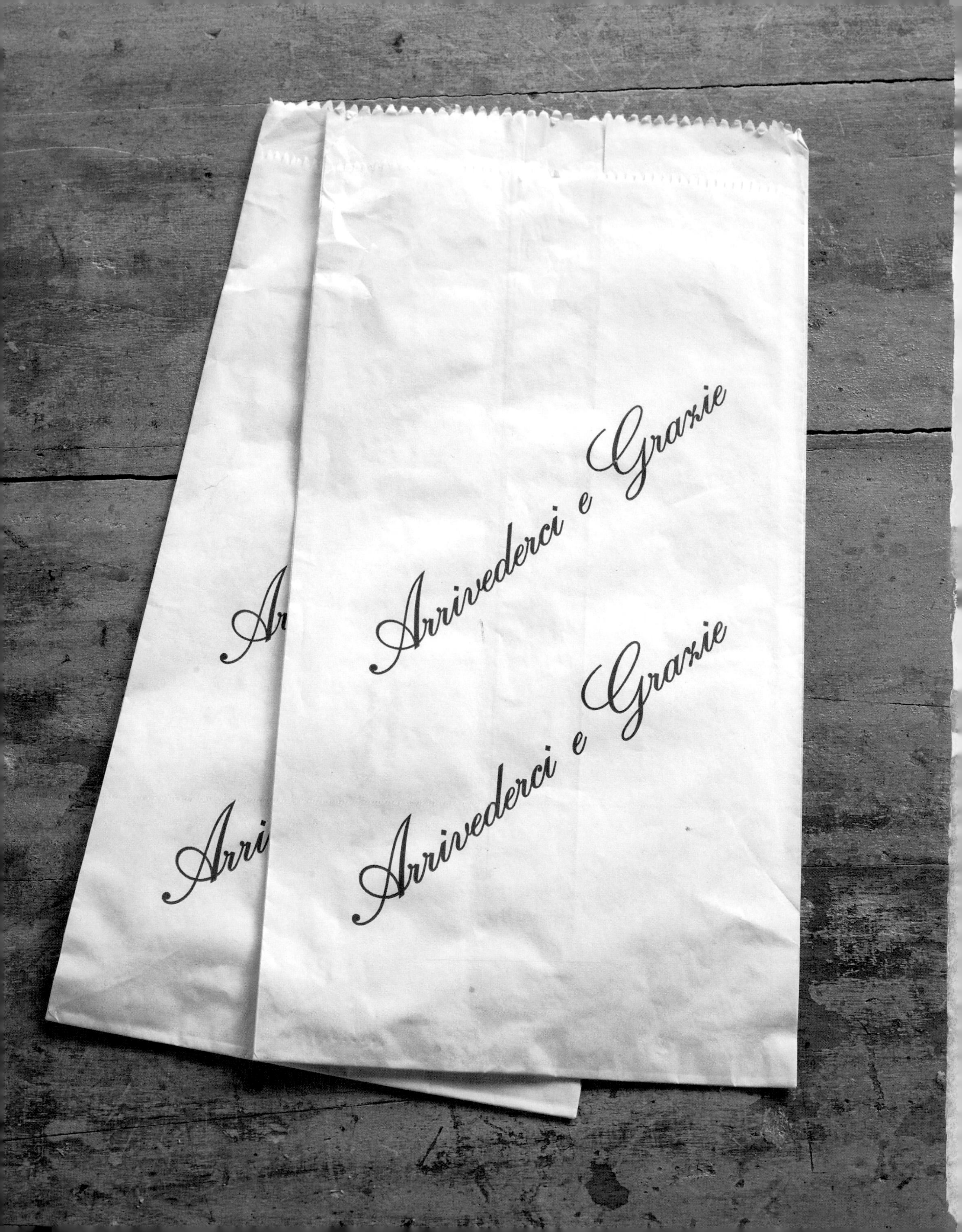
Arrivederci e Grazie
Arrivederci e Grazie